CROWN

MUSICAL INSTRUMENTS:
AN ILLUSTRATED HISTORY

ALEXANDER BUCHNER
MUSICAL INSTRUMENTS:
AN ILLUSTRATED HISTORY

CROWN

Alexander Buchner
MUSICAL INSTRUMENTS:
AN ILLUSTRATED HISTORY
Translated by Bořek Vančura
Graphic design Karel Drchal

© 1973 Artia, Prague
First published in the United States of America 1973 by Crown
Publishers, Inc.,
419 Park Avenue South, New York, New York 10016
Library of Congress Catalog Number 72 78328

Printed in Czechoslovakia

CONTENTS

H. S. Beham: Drummer and flute player

INTRODUCTION

Musical instruments are undoubtedly among the most ingenious of man's inventions. Take, for example, the violin — what an amazing and economical work of creation! With the possible exception of the scroll, nothing about the violin is merely decorative: everything has its own well-defined purpose; even the smallest part has its precise function. But despite the essentially functional character of its parts, the violin is an instrument of supreme elegance. This is less surprising when one considers how the shape of musical instruments has evolved through the centuries. Its evolution can be traced back to Mesolithic man, who may have tried to produce pleasant sounds by strumming on a bow. The culmination of this development is represented by violins made by masters from Cremona; Stradivari and Guarneri represent the peak of the art of violin-making. Even today their instruments remain unsurpassable ideals for violin-makers, who not only try to imitate them but also study very carefully their construction and the qualities of their sound.

From the very start man has attempted both to make an instrument with good sound qualities and at the same time to give it a shape that is pleasing to the eye. Thus, we may also regard musical instruments today as works of art. Almost all collections of musical instruments present and display each instrument from this viewpoint. Nothing evokes the sound of an instrument as vividly as the shape and design of the instrument itself. Musical scores represent an independent branch of the graphic arts, while portraits of outstanding musicians come within the sphere of painting. Musical instruments, on the other hand, just ask to be pictured and the sight of them immediately calls to mind a certain sound. Yet no other branch of musical knowledge has been so neglected as the history of musical instruments. It is not the aim of this book to solve the scientific problems of this knowledge. I have merely attempted to describe some of the extremely interesting and fascinating developments from prehistoric times up to the present day, from primitive prototype to highly evolved musical instrument. The majority of the relatively few available works on musical instruments do not contain sufficiently detailed illustrations. This book, on the other hand, describes the development of musical instruments in pictures, without lengthy text. The illustrations will speak for themselves to those who love the art of musical sound and the musical instruments that transform such sound into audible reality.

CAMPING SITE OF PREHISTORIC MAN

The first sound heralding the beginnings of musical history was heard many ages ago. It was produced by prehistoric man on an instrument that may have been a stringed or a wind instrument, or perhaps an idiophone. These first musical instruments, however, have not survived. They were destroyed shortly after being placed beside a dead person in his grave, or they may have been thrown away. The history of music therefore, in trying to trace the rise of musical instruments, must base all its theories upon scanty finds of prehistoric objects and upon the study of various types of instruments found today among primitive peoples whose musical culture is, at present, on the same level as that of prehistoric man.

Musical instruments are as old as man himself. They existed before any awareness of tonality or attempt to reproduce a particular melody. These early musical instruments produced sounds of a certain quality without any regard whatsoever to pitch. Yet even at this stage of development, when the instruments were an end in themselves, they achieved a considerable degree of refinement and variety.

We can learn something about music in prehistory from certain archeological finds of musical instruments. Those that have been discovered so far are certainly not numerous. They are mainly instruments made of materials which have successfully resisted the depredation of time, such as stone and bone. But research on them helps us to draw certain conclusions that advance our knowledge of the early stages of musical history. Among the earliest musical instruments used by man are undoubtedly *clappers*, *scrapers* and *rattles*. Their primary function was to drive away evil spirits or to assist in curing the sick, while later they were relegated to the role of toys for children. This theory is corroborated by the size of the earliest instruments, which clearly rules out any idea of their being used as toys. (A. Häusler: *Neue Funde steinzeitlicher Musikinstrumente in Osteuropa, Wissenschaftliche Zeitschrift der Martin Luther Universität Halle — Wittenberg*, June 1960 p. 321) Painted clappers from the beginning of the second millennium BC have been found in children's graves at Vychvatince in Moldavia (T. S. Passek: *Kratkie soobschenija Instituta istorii materialnoj kultury*, Moscow, 1956, p. 76). Clay figurines of various shapes with rattling stones inside were used in dances and rites, and also as toys for children. They have been found all over Europe, in Greece and Silesia, at settlements dating from the Hallstatt period, and a particularly large number of pieces come from the later La Tène age. The Stone Age also knew rattling instruments, as is evident from the scraper. The Paleolithic bone scraper found in the cave of Pekárna in Moravia has saw-like

teeth over which a plectrum was passed. A gong made of grey-green jade was found near Valencia in Venezuela, clear evidence that man very early in his history was able to distinguish various kinds of stones by the quality of the sound they produced. Besides these primitive instruments, prehistoric man was also acquainted with membrane musical instruments, some of them in a considerably advanced stage of development. The Bernburg goblet-shaped clay drums, as well as the spiral-shaped pottery drums, which look like binoculars and come from the southern part of the Soviet Union, are all from the Neolithic (Stone Age).

In 1953 archeologists found at the paleolithic site at Molodova (the Chernovice region in the USSR) a *flute* made from a hollowed piece of reindeer antler. This musical instrument is an outstanding example of prehistoric man's artistry and skill. The upper side is furnished with four and the bottom side with two holes which are spaced at wide intervals. It is also very interesting that the hollow does not go through the whole length of the antler, but reaches only as far as the fourth hole at the narrower end of the musical instrument. Thus we have a stopped flute producing sounds one octave lower than flutes that are open at both ends.

The considerable variety found in the category of flute instruments suggests that they have great importance in the cult of prehistoric man. Besides whistles and bone flutes, archeologists have also uncovered *Panpipes*, at the camping sites of prehistoric man which represent an important step forward in the development of musical instruments. The German musical scholar Curt Sachs wrote the following (Geist und Werden der Musikinstrumente, Berlin, 1931, p. 51): 'All musical instruments invented so far produced dull, screeching, howling, rattling or whining sounds; sometimes the instruments were combined into pairs, so that they produced the contrast between high and low pitch — but there is no trace of fixed tones or even of a scale. And into this purely ritual world of sound there penetrated a musical instrument whose qualities of sound, both with regard to pitch and to scale, made it acceptable to the majority of the world, an instrument that does not produce isolated shrieks or dull rustling sounds but gives forth an ordered scale of tones'.

But the find from Le Placard in Charent (O. Seewald: *Beiträge zur Kenntnis der steinzeitlichen Musikinstrumente Europas*, Vienna, 1934, pp. 36 ff), generally considered to be the oldest example of Panpipes, is still questionable, though the same is not true of another central European find from the late La Tène age. It comes from Klein-Kühnau near Dessau and was discovered in the ashes of an urn-grave (M. Ebert:

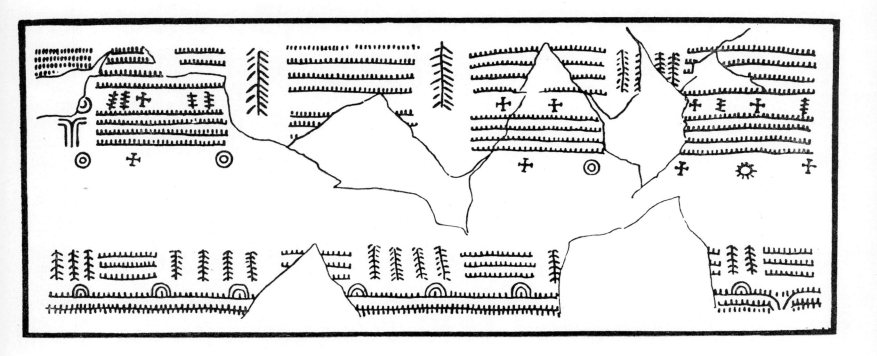

Reallexikon der Vorgeschichte, Berlin, 1929, vol. 8, p. 358). These are without any doubt Panpipes made of five reeds of various length and fastened together in a resin casing. A very important find of Panpipes was made in the southern Ukraine at the cemetery of hunters and fishermen (M. Makarenko: *Mariupilskij mogilnik*, Kiev, 1933). The object is dated circa 2000 BC and consists of seven or eight decorated pipes made of hollowed bird's bones. The shortest one measures 4 cm and the longest one 10 cm.

Prehistoric culture made great advances in the Bronze Age. In addition to edge and reed wind instruments there appeared the first prototypes of mouthpiece instruments. Considerable advances in metalworking made possible in the early Bronze Age the creation of bronze horns, modelled on animal horns. Of these the most highly developed musical instruments, both from the point of view of workmanship and the quality of sound, are the *lurs*, which have the shape of mammoth tusks. The lur measures from 150 cm to 240 cm, with the tube curving in a beautiful upward spiral and ending in a forward-turned bell. The tube consists of two parts of different size and has eyelets along the seam for hanging it from a chain. The mouthpiece is cast in one piece with the lower part of the tube and is very deep and cup-shaped, in later examples resembling the mouthpiece of a modern tenor trombone. The flat disc-like bell is often richly decorated. Both the mouthpiece and the bell are furnished with rings to which lozenge-shaped plates are attached. These plates reverberated to the sound of the lur and thus added a livelier timbre to it. It is generally assumed that lurs were used in rituals. This theory is borne out by the fact that they are most often found in peatbogs, at places where rituals took place. Peat is very good for preserving objects, so these elegant instruments are usually found in a very good state of preservation. With some exceptions lurs have mostly been found in pairs; both instruments are the same size and of the same pitch, but the tubes have curves winding in opposite ways, resembling bull's horns. On rock paintings lurs are sometimes arranged in twos or fours, with their tubes turned to the right and left. Most of them have been found in Danish peatbogs and are the pride of Scandinavian museums today. They are tuned in C and E flat, but also in D, E and G. In tests they produced seventeen harmonics, but their number could be increased to twenty-four.

With all due respect to the weight of archeological evidence — that is, preserved archeological finds — we may state that no experiments made with original or reconstructed musical instruments have so far proved the existence of a prehistoric tonality. Tonometric tests made with prehistoric flutes (these are mentioned by J. V. S. Megaw in his article 'The Earliest Musical Instruments in Europe', *Archaeology*, 21, no. 2, p. 125) show no evidence of any ordered tonality in prehistoric times. Similar result have been reached by John Coles in the course of tonometric tests on about thirty Irish horns.

It is an open question whether the origin of the musical bow, a very simple stringed instrument used by primitive peoples, should be sought in the hunting bow. But it is evident that a ring of strong spikes on the bell of Irish horns from the Bronze Age, which are blown on the side of the tube, in a similar way to African horns, was not only a musical instrument but at the same time a dangerous weapon. The Greek historian Diodorus Siculus speaks of Celtic bards accompanying their songs on stringed instruments resembling the Greek *lyre*, while an old Irish song describes a four-sided stringed instrument called a *crot*. This name calls to mind the ancient *cythar*, while the name *chrotta*, which is a Latinized form of crot, is mentioned

11

by the Venetian Fortunatus (*chrotta Britanna canat*). The Celtic wind instrument known as a *karnyx*, from the late Iron Age, depicted on the relief of a silver cauldron from Gundestrup, does not differ much from the Roman *lituus*. In speaking about the karnyx we are standing at the threshold of classical times, when many musical instruments were still on the same level as their prehistoric predecessors.

THE RISE AND FALL
OF ANCIENT CIVILIZATIONS

We may never know what music was like at the dawn of human history. The most remarkable musical relic— and perhaps one of the earliest depictions of musical instruments ever found — is a fragment of a lapis lazuli vase that comes from the excavations of a southern Babylonian temple in Bismaya. It dates from the third or even the fourth millennium BC, a period when the Sumerians ruled the regions along the Tigris and Euphrates rivers. The first of the musicians represented on the fragment plays a harp, which is very much like the arched harp used in Burma and Africa; the next has a similar instrument with a triangular soundbox and long tassels like the later Assyrian harps. But the most surprising thing about these instruments is the perfection of their construction, which must have been the result of a very long development. From the number of strings — the first instrument has seven, the second five strings — we can conclude that musicians at that time had already become acquainted with a five-note scale.

In addition to these lyre-shaped harps, which were held slanting and pressed to the body, *frame drums* were also used in court ceremonies. These were played only by women. Some of them are of tremendous size, as much as five feet in diameter. In Japanese and Chinese temples we can still see drums with their skins nailed on, like the Sumerian-Babylonian drums. Musical instruments in the strict sense of the word were represented by the eleven-string lyre, with a bull depicted on the edge of the body. It appears in this shape on a relief from the Sumerian royal palace at Tello. It is interesting to note that not so long ago the Georgians in the Caucasus used to play a harp with two horses and a bull carved in a circle. Another instrument was the lute, which had a small body and a long and narrow neck. It is carried by a shepherd on a clay fragment dating from the middle or end of the third millennium BC.

Few accounts concerning music in ancient Babylon are known, but it is still surprising to read the poem on Ishtar's journey to hell and notice its remarkable similarity to the later Greek myth of Orpheus. Nothing has so far been discovered about music and musical instruments in the Middle Kingdom. Not until the first millennium BC, with the appearance of the first Syrian and Hittite influences, do we find musical instruments depicted on stone reliefs: they include a short *trumpet*, a small *lyre*, a *lute* with two strings and a long neck, and also a double *oboe* and *cymbals*. The Turkish Archeological Museum in Ankara has a bas-relief depicting a guitar player. This instrument closely resembles a guitar depicted 2,700 years later in the Spanish codex of the *Cantigas de Santa Maria*.

In the centuries preceding our era Assyrian music reached its peak. Musicians were given privileged positions and ranked above court officials, immediately below the gods and the king. The voices of gods were often compared with the sound of musical instruments. Ishtar, for example, had a voice that was compared to a sweet flute, and Ramman, the wind-god, possessed a voice like the sound of an oboe. The Chaldean Empire, which followed after the Assyrian rule, knew so many musical instruments that the well-known passage in the Book of Daniel, calling upon the people to worship the golden image, gives a whole collection of instruments.

The earliest historical accounts of Egypt go as far back into the past as the beginning or even the end of the fourth millennium BC and reliefs dating from the Fourth Dynasty depict musical instruments at a considerably advanced stage of development. Musicians often played in groups and had *long flutes* and *arched harps*, while singers beat time by clapping their hands. The Old Kingdom also knew *frame drums* and wind instruments related to the clarinet. Paintings in a tomb near Beni Hassan prove that Syrian nomads brought the lyre to Egypt at the beginning of the second millennium BC. The repertory of musical instruments known in Egypt was extended sometime around 1500 BC, when the kings of the Eighteenth Dynasty conquered Asia Minor and the slaves coming to the Egyptian court brought with them their musical instruments. Of the original Egyptian instruments the *harp* continued to be used; the flute was replaced by

VNICA CHORDA QVA SONI CVIVSLIBET CONSONANTIÆ SIMVL AVDIRI POSSVNT.

its shriller counterpart, the Syrian *double clarinet* which, in a slightly modified form, is still used today by the Egyptian fellaheens, to whom it is known as *argul*. In addition to the arched harp there was the Asiatic angular harp and also lutes and trumpets. The popularity of the ancient Egyptian harp was so well established that the instrument could not easily be replaced, but the number of its strings was increased and the body enlarged. During the times of the Serap cult the repertory of these new wind and stringed instruments was completed by the introduction of hooked pipes, which probably came to Egypt from Asia, since the Greeks regarded them as a Phrygian invention, and hand drums. These drums were barrel-shaped and their primary function was to accentuate the rhythm.

In Egyptian temple music *clappers* and *rattles* were still used alongside the harp. But the most important instrument here was the *sistrum*, a kind of rattle whose function was similar to that of Catholic sacrament bells. This instrument, closely connected with the cult of Isis, lived on through ancient times and was introduced into all the Mediterranean lands. We can find its traces today not only in Abyssinia but as far away as the Caucasus. Egyptian music played outside the temples was subject to Syrian influences until the very end of the independent era of the Egyptian state and even the penetration of Greek and Roman cultures in the last three centuries BC did not outweigh Asiatic influence.

In Roman times the centre of Egyptian musical culture was in Alexandria, which became the melting-pot of Egyptian and Syrian traditions on the one hand and those of Greece on the other. In the Berlin Museum is an Egyptian terracotta figure of a musician wearing a Syrian cap and playing Panpipes. The instrument has a bag and a pipe leading from it to the boy's mouth, who is blowing the bag up. This curious arrangement is in fact a transitional stage between the bagpipes and the organ with bellows that had originated in Asia Minor. A sweeping revolution in the development of the organ came in the third century BC when the Alexandrian engineer Ktesibios perfected an air inlet and constructed the first water organ or *hydraulis*.

While architecture and sculpture are typical Greek arts and were of great importance for European art even as late as the Carolingian era, Greek music developed exclusively under foreign influences. Musical instruments of the ancient world, therefore, are only a part of the musical culture of those important nations in Asia who have kept their traditions alive up to the present time. No musical instrument is known to have originated on Greek soil and yet the importance of Greek music and the richness of musical life in Greece are remarkable. Music penetrated the whole of Greek society and played a major role in the education of youth, in rituals, in military life and in the private life of individuals. Philosophers pondered its ethical significance and its history was studied by many scholars.

Despite all this careful study, which was concerned more with ethics than aesthetics, the harp held by the Phaeacian singer Demodocus and the seven-stringed *kithara* played by Achilles in his tent prove that the Greeks found much pleasure in joyful and inspiring music. The kithara, whose name still lives today in the modern musical instrument known as the *zither*, belongs to the lyre family and occupied an important place in Greek music. Originally it had seven gut strings spanning the flat and rectangular soundbox,

Lodovico Fogliano
Musica theorica

13

which had two arms joined by a cross-piece; later, however, the number of strings was increased to eleven. Its origin must be sought in lyre-type instruments played in Egypt and Syria. The first historical account concerning the kithara is found in an ode by Terpander of 675 BC. Paintings on vases show two types of this instrument: the older one was held close to the body by a strap known as a *telamon*, while the later type was held upright, as can be seen for instance on classical representations of Apollo, Orpheus and Amphion, and the strings were struck with a plectrum.

The second most typical stringed instrument of Greece is the *lyre*, which gave its name to lyrical poets from the island of Lesbos. The lyre has its origin in Thrace. The body was in fact a tortoise-shell spanned with a piece of skin and two animal horns joined with a cross-piece. The construction was not as sophisticated as that of the kithara but it was easier to play. The lyre was therefore used mainly at home, in education and for entertainment. *Magadis* is a name that used to be given to two different types of instrument, one a stringed and the other a wind instrument. The stringed magadis was of Lydian origin and Anacreon was already acquainted with it. It had a triangular soundbox with twenty strings producing the ten fundamental notes and their respective octaves. The fundamental notes were produced by the left hand and the octaves by the right, without the use of a plectrum. Some earlier theories assumed that this type of magadis was identical with the *pektis* invented by Sappho, but recently scholars have come to believe that it is only related to it.

The wind magadis may have been a variety of the *aulos*. We have some evidence proving that both types of magadis were played together, but the most important wind instrument was certainly the aulos. According to early legends the mythical singer Olympus brought it from Phrygia to Greece. The first virtuoso to play it was Sakadas of Argos, who in 586 BC won a prize at the Delphi Games for an instrumental poem about Apollo's fight against the dragon Python. Because of its shrill tone this instrument was regarded as barbaric and excluded by scholars from musical education, for they claimed that it was harmful to the soul. Originally three fingerholes produced the tones of the tetrachord, but later more of them were made to enable the musician to play octaves and twelfths. When playing on the aulos at concerts the musicians wore broad straps across their mouths, which were known as *phorbeia* or halters. The straps prevented air escaping from either side of the players' mouths, and at the same time concealed any grimaces they might make when blowing really hard. They generally used a double pipe, and therefore the Greeks used the plural — *auloi*. The pipes had a double reed and their lengths differed slightly. The use of a double pipe served to increase the sound volume; the right pipe played the melody while the left one accompanied it on a higher note. This instrument has never been made of metal but we do know of some auloi from Roman times. These were found in Athens and Pompeii and have a kind of stop arrangement that made a wider range of tones possible. Auloi were also used in the orgiastic cult of Hellenistic Rome; for this reason they were condemned by the Church and in the fifth century AD they disappeared altogether from Christian territories.

The *syrinx* or *Panpipes*, made up of a row of reed pipes of varying lengths, was a folk instrument and the same is true of the *keras*, or animal horn. *Salpinx* was the name for the military trumpet made of metal. Among the numerous rattling and percussion instruments were a hand-drum, the *tympanon*, and some kind of castanets fastened to the feet, known as the *scabellum*. It was in fact a loose sole, made of wood, on the sandal of the chorus leader, with which he beat time. The *cymbal* recalls a one-handed flute with a drum; it is a bowl fixed to a flexible metal rod and struck against another metal disc, while the other hand played a wind instrument.

In the middle of the second century BC the Romans conquered Greece and thus became the immediate successors to the culture of Alexandria, but they no longer believed in the educational power of music and therefore paid less attention to it than the Greeks. Plato's musical ethics were replaced by the formalism of Epicurus, which was clearly formulated by Cicero. He held the view that music could not be of any real benefit to man, but supplied him only with childish amusement; and this in turn was useless, for it did not point the way to spiritual happiness. From this particular angle we must judge all that Rome contributed to the development of musical instruments. The music of imperial Rome, already showing signs of decadence, was completely under the influence of Greek musicians and Greek musical instruments, which were slowly succumbing to an ethos of megalomania. Lyres, for instance, were as big as litters, as we know from the writings of Martianus Capella, and orchestras reached such enormous proportions that Seneca reckoned to see more performers than members of the audience in the theatre.

Roman music differs from Greek music in that it used more Roman wind instruments. Wherever music was performed in Rome there appeared first of all the *tibia* — a single reed pipe, probably of Etruscan origin. Like the aulos the tibia was also doubled, the right pipe being shorter than the left and with a proportionally higher tone. The tibia, however, was later supplanted by the aulos, a change that was due mainly to the influence of Greek music.

The most important group of musical instruments was the brass, which played a dominant role in Roman military music — the only musical field in which the Romans surpassed the Greeks. The chief signal instrument of the infantry was the *tuba*. This was a straight trumpet with a widening tube and funnel-shaped bell. The tuba was in fact the counterpart of the Greek salpinx. The cavalry used a hooked trumpet known as the *lituus*, while the *buccina* was a signal horn made almost in a circle. A Celtic invention, a trumpet with the tube turned at right angles and terminating in a fantastic dragon's head, was called a *karnyx*. It is interesting to see that this shape was revived in France at the beginning of the nineteenth century in the bass horn, which developed from the bass serpent. All of these musical instruments usually accompanied gay marching in triumphal parades.

Stringed instruments occured much less frequently among the Romans. The art of playing the kithara was taken over from the Greeks. Dionysius Halicarnasus informs us that in ancient liturgical rites the Romans also played, in addition to the tibia, a seven-stringed lyre known as the *barbita*. The only instrument that the Romans did perfect was the *hydraulis* — the organ in which, unlike the pneumatic organ, the air pressure was regulated in the windchest by a column of water. This explains the frequent use of the name water organ, which is certainly not correct. Soon the hydraulis became indispensable to Roman musical life, and by the time of the collapse of the Roman Empire it occupied a leading position among musical instruments. It appeared not only at the court of the Emperor Nero but also in the circus, where it accompanied gladiator fights, being played with other wind instruments. In the west it was slowly falling into oblivion but in the eastern part of the Roman Empire it continued to be played for a long time. The last mention of the hydraulis is found in a poem by Leo Magister written in the sixth century AD, which praises the baths of Byzantium. Then it was replaced for good by the pneumatic organ.

M. Konáč of Hodištkov: On the Lamentation of Justice

FIDDLING ANGELS

From the very outset Christianity was in favour of vocal music and strongly opposed to instrumental music. The result of this attitude is not difficult to guess: the natural development of musical instruments came to a complete standstill and in many cases they were relegated to the role of signal instruments. For many centuries the organ was considered an instrument of luxury, coming from the court of the emperors of the eastern part of the Roman Empire, and it was even asserted that the devil's voice sounded from the organ pipes. When the organ at last found its way into churches it was used to accompany vocal music only.

The few remaining classical instruments were played only by minstrels and itinerant entertainers. On the other hand, all the musical instruments mentioned in the Old Testament — particularly the harp of David — enjoyed great reverence, though they had never been seen by anyone. An illustration in an illuminated English manuscript of the twelfth century contrasts instruments condoned by the Church with those that were denounced, even contrasting God's musicians with the Devil's music-makers, who were described as Satan's sacristans and compared with wild beasts. Among the approved instruments were the *monochord*, *chimes*, *Panpipes*, *organ*, *harp* and *cornett*, while the *rebec*, *horn* and *drums* were the Devil's instruments and only fit to accompany beardances and tumblers (plate 42).

A number of instruments were still used, as we can clearly see from medieval paintings and sculpture, which also record the social function of these instruments. Many of them were used to accompany folk songs and dances, as well as religious polyphonic vocal music. But the musical instruments that have actually been preserved are extremely rare. The oldest specimens in big museums of musical instruments mainly date from the sixteenth century. Thus there is a time-gap of some ten to eleven centuries in our knowledge of the development of musical instruments, from ancient finds to these late medieval relics. The music historian will find the period of the migration of peoples one of the least informative chapters in musical history. Illuminated manuscripts, almost the only existing source of information about musical instruments, rarely date to before the ninth century AD, at which time the very important formative period in the development of European musical instruments was already over. This particular period witnessed the first acceptance of types of musical instruments brought from the East, the first revival of the antique repertory of musical instruments (aulos, kithara, hydraulis), which had lost their vitality and may have even outlived their usefulness. The only relic from the period of the migration of peoples is the Avaric double pipe found near Jánoshida in Hungary. (D. Bartha: *Die awarische Doppelschalmei von Jánoshida*, Budapest, 1934). This double pipe points quite clearly to the existence of eastern influences upon European instruments in the early Middle Ages. Even if this pipe eventually proves to be of Slavonic origin (it is actually a reed wind instrument) it will still remain a very important piece of evidence, showing that many double pipes known from illustrations and considered up to the present time to be double flutes are in fact a type of double clarinet brought from the East.

It can justly be asserted that no medieval instrument was native to Europe: all of them were imported from Asia. This migration did not take place in any clear-cut period of time, but occurred gradually, at various times and along various routes. The most important route was via Byzantium and North Africa. Illustrations dating from before the ninth century were still influenced by classical culture and the instruments depicted therefore echo the Greek and Roman repertory, as we can see in the Bible of Charles the Bald. Even the Utrecht psalter, which is our first important source of information on musical instruments, is not entirely free from the influences of classical antiquity. The organ depicted is actually a hydraulis and even the chrotta is fairly close to the kithara. Among the wind instruments of the early Middle Ages we find, in addition to large military horns and elegantly carved oliphants made of ivory, small horns with fingerholes, which represent the earliest form of the cornett family that became so popular in the sixteenth and seventeenth centuries. Of the flutes, the Panpipes were used along with the double pipe.

In the sixth century Bishop Isidore of Seville left us a very interesting work on celestial music, the illustrations for which became a very popular subject for many medieval artists. It is only natural that the celestial orchestra included all musical instruments known at that time, played by angels and spirits of saints. The *musica coelestis* inspired the imagination of many artists, for example those who executed the sculptured decoration on church portals, some of which depicted figures playing various musical instruments. This iconographical material confirms the importance of musical instruments in medieval music, which was mainly performed by jongleurs and minnesingers. A Provençal jongleur of the thirteenth century had to be versed in all these accomplishments: 'Player, you must be acquainted with nine instruments, fiddle, bagpipes, pipe, harp, hurdy-gurdy, jig, tenstring, psaltery and chrotta. If you learn them well you are able to meet all demands. Also, let the lyre sound and the bells tinkle'. This enumeration of instruments confirms the view of the musicologist Johann de Grocheo, who wrote in his tractate *Theoria* (Cod. 2663 in the Darmstadt Library): 'The most important among the musical instruments seem to be stringed instruments, especially the fiddle, because it can play a song and in fact any other musical form'. The importance of the fiddle is also evident from medieval illustrations. Second only to the harp of David, it is the most frequently depicted instrument. It very probably originated in Central Asia, as we can see from the earliest type, which was in the shape of a spade and was held in the oriental manner. A fiddle like this appears on ivory book covers dating from the eighth century (A. Goldschmidt: *Die Elfenbeinskulpturen aus der romanischen Zeit*, Berlin, 1926, pp. 34 ff) as well as in the manuscript Utrecht psalter of the ninth century. The oval type of fiddle appeared for the first time in the tenth century. Alongside the oval fiddle the Slavs began to develop in the tenth century a new, and as it subsequently proved, final shape of the fiddle with a narrow and waisted body. The instrument was rather big and awkward to handle, so it had a strap and was slung over the shoulder. The Manesse Codex (Heidelberg, University Library) shows, in addition to this fiddle, an instrument that was about half its size. This small fiddle was especially popular in Italy, where it was perfected by adding a drone string.

A typical stringed instrument of the Middle Ages was the *hurdy-gurdy*. The main feature of its construction is a revolving disc placed in the lower part of the body, which touched the strings and thus produced sounds. To stop the strings the hurdy-gurdy had a key mechanism with a few frets built in the neck of the instrument. The disc made possible a continuous sound while the keyboard provided melodic possibilities. Early illustrations show that the hurdy-gurdy was of a considerable size and was therefore played by two musicians sitting next to each other and holding the instrument on their knees. One of them turned the disc while the other manipulated the keyboard. This is the kind of hurdy-gurdy seen on twelfth-century sculptures on the archivolts of the western portal of St. Dominic's at Soria and in the cathedral in Santiago de Compostela. Later the cumbersome tangent mechanism was replaced and the body of the instrument could be made much smaller. Thus the hurdy-gurdy became easily portable and because no special skills were needed in its construction it soon turned out to be a very popular folk instrument. Its old name, *organistrum*, was in the course of time replaced by new ones, *armonium* and *symphonium*. In the fourteenth century the popularity of the hurdy-gurdy faded, for it could hold its own as a musical instrument only as long as musical idiom was based on organ point (drone accompanied melody). In the course of further development the hurdy-gurdy lost its place in instrumental music and today it survives only as a folk instrument in some European countries.

Besides the hurdy-gurdy the *Trumscheit, tromba*

marina or *trumpet marine* is the only instrument that has not undergone any major changes in the many centuries of its existence. Its characteristic feature is a very long and narrow pyramidal body whose length made flageolet technique possible at one end. The bridge of the tromba marina rested with one foot on the soundboard, while the other foot touched it only lightly. The vibrations of this shorter and thinner foot gave the sound of the tromba marina a characteristic timbre. The bow did not touch the string above the bridge, as is usual with all other instruments played with the bow, but in the upper part of the instrument, between the scroll and the musician's left thumb, which stopped the strings. Medieval illustrations also show the rather unusual way of holding the instrument, which resembles the way in which a trumpet was held. Does this unusual and certainly uncomfortable position explain its name? Or is it in any way connected with the fact that it was possible to play on this

Gafurius:
Theorica musice

17

L. degli Uberti:
Martialis,
Epigrammata

instrument by means of the flageolet technique, the same natural scale as on the trumpet?

Typologically medieval stringed instruments may be divided into two main categories. The first includes three-part, or fiddle-type, instruments with the soundbox consisting of soundboard, back and sides. In the second category belong instruments of the lute family, with the soundbox constructed of two parts — a flat soundboard and a convex back. The two-part instruments were mostly plucked with fingers or a plectrum, while many of the three-part instruments were played with a bow. The most important of the two-part instruments is the lute, though it is not known when and how the lute reached the continent of Europe. On various illustrations the lute can easily be confused with other plucked instruments, such as the *rubeba*, *cobza*, *mandora* or *quinterne*. True lutes with a set-off neck, frets and a slanted peg-box appear for the first time in medieval illustrations in the fourteenth century, and the names *laudis*, *leutus* and *lutana* are not much older. At first the body was pear-shaped, but later Italian lute-makers changed it to an almond shape. The back was made of narrow strips of maple wood and in the Renaissance period, which represents the heyday of the lute, it was even made of precious cypress and sandal wood. Many outstanding works of art have survived to testify to the beauty of the lute, from Giotto's sculptures on the Campanile in Florence to Van Dyck's famous 'Lute-player'.

In the whole hierarchy of musical instruments none has more right to be called 'royal' than the *harp*. In the Middle Ages it was as closely connected with King David as Jubal with the anvil or Pythagoras with the monochord. In the early Middle Ages Irish musicians acquainted the peoples of Europe with the wide Irish harp, which later became a model for a similar, though smaller, instrument. This small harp found much

popularity with French jongleurs and German minnesingers. Together with the Provençal culture there came to the north poets and musicians who sang and played various musical instruments, and the small harp certainly enjoyed the greatest favour among them. It appears in this particular shape in all medieval illustrations and it was frequently referred to in all literary works.

From the ninth to the sixteenth centuries the size of the harp changed only very slightly. In illustrations it rarely reaches above the head of the musician, who played it seated. But there also existed smaller harps, with a strap and slung round the neck, which the musician played standing. These harps usually had extended snake-shaped necks which rested on the player's shoulder. This instrument was much favoured by troubadours and minnesingers to accompany their songs. There was scarcely a single novel or poem in the age of chivalry that did not describe the sound of the harp, or in which the account of military adventure was not introduced by a harp-player. In medieval illustrations King David is frequently depicted with the harp but also with a plucked instrument whose Latin name, *nabulum* or *decacordum*, appeared as early as the fifth century in the tractate *De Musica* by A. M. Boethius.

In the late Middle Ages the name *psaltery* was introduced. Up to the ninth century the psaltery was usually deltoid in shape, but later its shape changed frequently according to the countries in which it was made. In the Middle Ages the psaltery was introduced into the sphere of folk music, the strings were struck and under the name *salterio tedesco* it became the precursor of the present-day cymbalum. The modern repertory of musical instruments is indebted to the psaltery for the origin of stringed keyboard instruments. A psaltery with a keyboard with the strings plucked is known as a *clavicembalo*, while the instrument with tangents was called a *clavichord* or *manicordion*. The triangular shape is also characteristic of the piano, whose birth at the beginning of the eighteenth century was influenced by all the instruments that had developed from the psaltery.

In addition to the psaltery there also existed in the Middle Ages what were known as *half psalteries*, which arose by truncating the trapezoid shape of the instrument. This is well expressed by the old French names *micamon* and *michanon* in the poem *Remède de la Fortune* by Guillaume de Machault (1300—77), (G. de Machault, *Oeuvres*, Paris, 1911, II, p. 145). If the slanting side of the half-psaltery was curved the instrument had the shape of a wing and was therefore called by the Latin name *ala*. The alas depicted in Bohemian medieval manuscripts, such as the Passional of the Abbess Kunhuta, in Velislav's Bible, in the Bible of King Wenceslas IV and in the mural paintings at the Karlštejn Castle near Prague, are typically Czech and were therefore called *ala bohemica* (*Cancellaria Johannis Noviforensis episcopi olomucensis*, published by F. Tadra, Vienna, 1886, No. 128, pp. 103 ff).

The Middle Ages also knew an instrument which was a combination of harp and psaltery. In early manuscripts it goes by various Latin names, such as *tympanon, nablum, kithara* and many others. So far it is known from Bohemian illustrations only. It may be described as a psaltery harp, with the body consisting of two soundboxes. The first one had soundholes in the soundboard or in the sides and held about sixteen strings. The other soundbox, in the shape of a wide curving strip with the soundhole in the middle, occupied the space between the first one and the neck, but not the whole space, so that the shortest strings were not above the soundbox. A painting at Karlštejn Castle depicting an old man from the Apocalypse is a very valuable source of information on the construction and shape of this psaltery harp.

Medieval wind instruments included some types that had been represented in the prehistoric repertory, such as the Panpipes, flute and animal horn with fingerholes. The shape of the Panpipes, as we know it from the Middle Ages, is the result of influences exerted by the oriental *zamr* during the crusades. French literary sources from the twelfth century speak of a musical instrument known as *chalamelle* or *chalemie* (from the Latin *calamus*). Period illustrations show two kinds of medieval Panpipes. One of them, depicted in the Manesse Codex, has a short and slightly conical body, while the other — as we can see on a Gothic panel painting by Paolo Veneziano called *Coronation of the Virgin Mary* (Prague, National Gallery) — is longer and more slender.

We have very little information on the flute before the year 1500. The earliest illustration shows it in perpendicular position and with a cylindrical body — this is a French miniature from the eleventh century in the Bibliothèque Nationale in Paris. Its sound was so delicate that in France it was called the sweet flute (*flûte douce*). It reached Europe from Asia by way of North Africa, but also via Hungary and Bohemia. The Slavs may have contributed to the development of this instrument, as is proved by the *Bohemian flute* (*fluste de Behaigne*) mentioned in early French literature. A frequent figure in medieval illustrations is that of a musician playing the flute with one hand and a small drum with the other. From the poem *Frauendienst* by Ulrich von Lichtenstein we learn that the homeland of this inseparable pair of musical instruments was France, and that later they found their way to all corners of Europe. Machault in 'Le temps pastour' (*Oeuvres*, I, p. 53) calls them by the names *tabour* and *flaios* and goes on to say that there were more than twenty kinds of flutes, 'both powerful and weak' (tant de fortes comme de legières). Among the *flaios* Machault lists *fistule, pipe, souffle* and *frétiau;* the latter was later renamed *galoubet*. Up to the fourteenth century the one-hand flute had a short body, but later it became longer and narrower and was given a head. Despite the fact that the one-hand flute had only two tone-holes on the upper side and one on the under side it was possible, with the help of the natural harmonic series of overtones, to play on it a scale encompassing two octaves.

All horns with fingerholes made of other materials than animal horn are called *cornetts*. This instrument was frequently used in the later Renaissance period, mainly because strict Guild regulations permitted only musicians who were in the service of the nobility or the church to use it. A really indispensable musical instrument of the Middle Ages was the trumpet. Musicians blew their trumpet at the castle to ask for bread or water, while in towns the sound of a trumpet heralded the presence of a nobleman, opened and concluded markets, announced the opening and closing of town gates. The trumpet had a very important role in army life. There were many varieties — for the cavalry, for fortified towns and castles, for the navy and warships. In principal, however, there were only two fundamental types, called by the Latin names *tuba* and *buccina*. The buccina had a conical tube without a bell and therefore resembled a bugle or a horn. The tuba, on the other hand, was cylindrical and had a flaring bell. The effort to produce ever higher harmonies led to the lengthening of the tube, which was consequently difficult to hold and easily damaged. From the fourteenth century the tubes of brass instruments were therefore turned and twisted into various shapes, until finally in the fifteenth century the shape resembled the letter S. This was also the beginning of a celebrated period of trumpeters, who played musical instruments called the *tromba clarina* or simply *clarina*, and who occupied privileged positions with the overlords and nobility.

With the end of ovations to Roman emperors at the Capitol and celebrations in honour of pagan deities in temples, the musical instruments which had played such an important role on these occasions of pomp and glory were also silenced and forgotten. Most of the musical instruments of the Greeks and Romans disappeared and fell into oblivion. Some instruments used in the fifth century for religious, military and artistic purposes are mentioned in a letter by St Jerome to Dardanus (*Epistola Hieronymi de Carminibus ad Dardanum*, London, British Museum, sign. Patrol lat., XXX, col. 213). The letter speaks of twelve instruments and the organ with fifteen bronze pipes is mentioned first. It is a well-known fact in the history of music that the Byzantine emperor Constantine VI Copronymos contributed to a great extent to the development of the pneumatic organ in Europe. In 757 he sent to Compiègne as a gift to king Pépin the Short an organ with pipes made of lead (Monument. Germ., p. 140). This was a small portable organ, called the *portative*, which had a strap and was carried in processions slung on the shoulder. With the right hand the musician played on the keys, while with the left hand he worked a bellows placed on the back of the instrument. When it was not necessary to carry the instrument it was placed on the player's left knee or on the table. The portative had anything from eight to thirty-two pipes made of various metals.

19

Each pipe had its own key, or rather a slidevalve, which was moved to and from while the back part of the valve opened and closed the air inlet to the pipes. Because of its limited range of tones the portative was only a subsidiary instrument in church music and served to intone Gregorian hymns. After reaching its heyday in the fourteenth and fifteenth centuries the portative experienced a sudden decline and was replaced by a much larger instrument, the *positive*.

The assertion that drums played only an unimportant role in medieval music (C. Sachs: *Musik-instrumentenkunde*, Leipzig, 1920, p. 96) is disproved by written as well as pictorial evidence. As early as the year 600 Isidore of Seville described a drum called a *symphonium* as a hollowed piece of wood covered on both sides with skin (*Originum sive etymologiarum libri* XX). In the illuminated manuscript 'Liber viaticus' of Jan of Středa we find a drum, its size corresponding approximately to that of the modern small drum, slung round the player's neck. The musician is striking it with two sticks which are at the correct angle of about 75 degrees to the skin. The right elbow of the player is raised in the same manner as today. Drums are mentioned by Machault in *The Conquest of Alexandria* under the comprehensive name of *tabours*, while kettle-drums are described as *naquairs*. The oriental origin of kettle-drums is also suggested by the Italian version of these instruments, which are called *naccherone*. Kettle-drums were widespread in Europe in the fifteenth century, but they were small. Larger instruments were imported from the western regions of Asia as late as the end of the eighteenth century. Kettle-drums were used in pairs, one kettle being always smaller than the other. Thus we can see that the Middle Ages knew all the main types of drums that are used in our orchestras today. Because the drums were frequently used in the army, and there the volume of sound was of primary importance, fairly large drums called *bedons* were also introduced in medieval times.

Of the idiophones medieval musicians were familiar only with *bells*, *jingle-bells*, *cymbals* and the *triangle*. On miniatures we can often see small bells held by musicians or suspended from a stand, which were struck with small hammers. In Latin texts they are described as *cymbalum* or *tintinnabulum*. A set of bells made up the chimes. The chimes were often used in church music; they were especially important, together with the organ, in sequences, because they lent to medieval music a mystical air. Among the instruments that were not subject to any strict theoretical principles but were still considered to be of noble tune was the triangle. Its Latin name is *tripos colybaeus* and two types were known — one in the shape of an isosceles triangle, the other as a trapezium. In a manuscript of St Emmeram dating from the tenth century (Munich, State Library, Cim. 14523) it is depicted in the shape of an open-work tripod. In the Middle Ages people found the sound of jingle-bells so joyful that they used to set these small bells tinkling at every possible occasion. They were so popular and fashionable that many people even sewed them onto their clothes. The clear sound of bells, jingle-bells and triangles achieved great popularity after the Crusades, when soldiers brought them home from the east.

Fiddles were usually made of one piece of wood and produced sound of very low volume. It is not surprising, therefore, that the Czech scholar Pauli Paulirini de Praga in his tractate on music of 1460, considered the harp to be the stringed instrument with the highest sound-volume. The sound-volume of large organs such as that of Winchester was thought to be unbearably loud in the Middle Ages, though it stands no comparison with modern instruments. Attempts at the introduction of whole consorts of instruments, each with a characteristic timbre, into the orchestra began as late as the end of the Middle Ages. In order to reach the lowest tone-hole in larger instruments, instrument-makers introduced the key for the first time in the fifteenth century. This revolutionary invention was of such importance for the further development of all wind instruments that in the Renaissance period they experienced unprecedented popularity.

CAPELLA DOMINORUM DE ROSIS

In the Renaissance instrumental music was for the first time distinguished from vocal music and was established as an independent branch of musical life in its own right. This development was partly due to church choirs, but mainly to numerous bands playing at the courts or seats of the nobility. The number of instruments found in these bands is surprising. Some accounts tell us that the band at the Berlin Court had seventy-two instruments in 1582 and the orchestra of the Dukes of Tyrol at the Ambras Castle near Innsbruck consisted of 186 instruments. The court orchestras of the Habsburg emperors Ferdinand I (1526—46), Maxmilian II (1564—76), and especially Rudolph II (1576—1612) certainly ranked high, and under the Emperor Rudolph II, Prague even became for a time the centre of European musical life.

It is in Bohemia that we find at the end of the sixteenth century an instrumental orchestra of very high quality, whose importance reached even beyond the borders of its homeland. This was an orchestra of the Rožmberk family known as the *Capella Dominorum de Rosis* — the orchestra of the Lords of the Rose. It was established by Vilém of Rožmberk in the town of Český Krumlov in 1552 (Václav Březan: *The Last of Rožmberk*, Prague, 1941), and reached the climax of its activity under Petr Vok, who died in 1611. This orchestra, vying with that of the emperor's court in the number of its musicians as well as in the variety of its instruments, became for the last time a dazzling picture of the pomp and musical glamour found at the castles of medieval nobility. Its repertory contained mainly French and Italian works: beautiful motets by Pierro Serton, a disciple of the famous musician Josquin Des Près, madrigals by the conductor Melchior Franck, who lived in Coburg, and works of Dutch composers who lived at the Prague court. The most interesting among them was Philippe de Monte, conductor of the court orchestra under Emperor Maxmilian and later under Rudolph II. No less important were the organ-players of Rudolph's orchestra: Charles Luyton, whose compositions heralded the arrival of the new Baroque style, Jacobus Regnart, a French master of polyphony, and the Slovenian composer Jacobus Handl-Gallus.

The fact that the orchestra of the Lords of the Rose used various combinations of musical instruments is clear evidence of the growing interest in the colour, contrast and blend of timbres, as a vital part of music. This interest had a far reaching influence on the construction of musical instruments. Written material, pictures, and, for the first time, the instruments themselves, give us a reasonably accurate idea of what an orchestra at that time was like. One fact is immediately interesting: the Middle Ages are characterized by the preponderance of stringed instruments, while the Renaissance revelled in a profusion of wind instruments of various constructions. Most of them were woodwinds unlike earlier periods, when wind instruments were represented mainly by brass instruments and only a handful of instruments of the flute and reed types.

The ever-increasing need for deeper tones led to the construction of very large instruments, which were very cumbersome for those who played them. But the most interesting thing about the Renaissance orchestra is the construction of the same musical instrument in several sizes. Thus it was quite possible for a descant member of one family to be lower in pitch than the bass member of a different family. These numerous instruments formed groups characterized by the same timbre. As an example we may mention a set of twenty-one recorders, which is also quoted by Praetorius.

In 1812 a very interesting find was made at the town of Jindřichův Hradec, the former seat of the Lords of the Rose. In an old junk-room in the former Jesuit College fourteen unusually large musical instruments were found. They were identified as late as 1952 by the present author, who also proved that they used to belong to the orchestra of the Lords of the Rose. They include five *pommers*, five *windcap-shawms*, a *double-bass crumhorn*, a *double-bass viol* and a *regal*. An inventory of the Rožmberk orchestra of 1610 (deposited in Jindřichův Hradec) lists even more musical instruments which were probably taken away by Swedish armies in 1622, such as recorders, cornetts, schryaris, lutes and viols, as well as a whole archive containing precious musical material.

The pommer occupied a very important place among the wind instruments of the Renaissance, as we can see not only from numerous illustrations but also from the number of instruments that have been preserved. The earliest illustration is in the chronicle of the Constance Council, of 1440, the work of Ulrich Richenthal. But the pommer was mentioned by musical theorists only after it had developed into its numerous varieties, ranging from the small shawm called the *bombardo sopranino* to the double-bass pommer named the *bombardone*. At the climax of its development the pommer had seven uncovered holes and several more with keys made of brass protected by the fontanelles. The lower part of the instrument was slightly flaring and the rim of the bell was protected against damage by a decorated metal ring. Marin Mersenne (*Harmonie universelle*, Paris, 1636) speaks of only three types of pommer: *dessus*, *taille* and *basse*. These instruments were extremely unwieldy, the double-bass pommer reaching a length of 8 feet 4 inches, so that in the course of the seventeenth century they gradually lost popula-

21

the musician blows very hard. The same principle was used for the construction of *rackets*. They have a very short body, so that a descant instrument measured only about four inches. In the short but thick body are nine interconnected channels and the surface is pierced with many holes, eleven of them tone-holes. Rackets had the same drawbacks as the sorduns: low sound volume and a tone that was not very well defined. But with their bent channels both rackets and sorduns pointed the way to the further development of wind instruments, such as the bassoon.

An important place in Renaissance music was given to wooden wind instruments, which had the reed placed in a windcap. When the bladder of a bladder-pipe was replaced by a wooden windcap it became the *crumhorn*. Nearly all names for this instrument refer to its crooked shape, only the Italian and Polish names — *cornamuto torto* and *szhort* — suggest that its sound was weaker than that of the pommer, mainly because of its narrow cylindrical channel. The origin of the crumhorn goes a long way back, but the earliest illustrations are from 1510, when Vittore Carpaccio painted his picture *Twelve-year old Jesus* with an angel playing one. The instrument did not even survive the Baroque period and in Germany, for example, belonged at that time to the group known as 'rust-eaten instruments' (verrostete Instrumente). In France, however, they lived on right down to the middle of the eighteenth century, though their construction was changed and they received a new name — the *tournebout*.

The windcap is again a characteristic feature of that type of shawm which retained its original marks — a short conical body and a wide channel. Under the German name *Rauschpfeife* this instrument entered the history of music on a woodcut by Hans Burgkmair of the famous 'Triumphal Procession of Emperor Maxmilian'. Somewhat earlier is an illustration of this instrument in the Czech printed *Tractate on Happiness* by Hynek of Poděbrady. At the present time only the collections in Prague and Berlin still contain specimens of windcap shawms. A study of them enables us to establish a whole family of six windcap shawms, from the soprano to the double-bass ones. Because of the wide channel and conical tube, the sound of windcap shawms was dull and inexpressive. Overblowing was impossible and therefore the compass was limited to the tones produced by the tone-holes and one key. Consequently the windcap shawms were not suited to the rendering of ever more sophisticated compositions and were probably used only during the first few decades of the sixteenth century. Thus it is not surprising that the author of the Rožmberk inventory lists, dating from the beginning of the seventeenth century, was not able to recall their correct name.

The recorder, which was not yet challenged by the cross flute, also developed during the Renaissance into a variety of sizes, ranging from the small flute mentioned by Praetorius to a double-bass instrument with a brass mouthpipe in the shape of the letter S. Praeto-

rity and their place was taken by the *bassoon*. The theorists of the eighteenth century do not know them at all.

A liking for deep tones and the endeavour to compress the tube of the instrument into the smallest possible space led to the development of wooden wind instruments of unusual construction. One of them is the *sordun*, a picture of which may be seen on the frontispiece of Praetorius's *Theatrum instrumentorum* (Wolfenbüttel, 1618), in the hands of a musician to the right of the organ. Four sorduns can be seen in the Kunsthistorisches Museum in Vienna, originally part of the collection from Ambras Castle. These unique specimens have the channel bent three times in the body and are carefully turned from a piece of boxwood. Though the double-bass sordun produced the lowest tone of double-bass E_1, it is a relatively small instrument. But it has a very low volume of sound, which does not go beyond mezzopiano, even when rius enumerates a whole family of recorders consisting of twenty one instruments: two small recorders, two descant ones tuned one fourth lower, two descant ones tuned one fifth lower, four alto ones, four tenor ones, four bass ones, one bass and one double-bass recorder. In the sixteenth century there was no fixed system for tuning the musical instruments. Fétis, for example, writes about recorders of the same type but with different tuning and mentions a descant flute tuned a major third lower than other instruments of the same size (*Fabrications des Instruments de Musique*, Paris, 1855). Praetorius also complained that well-tuned recorders were extremely rare. He therefore recommended that the instrument be made in two parts, one of which could be telescoped into the other. When instrument-builders criticized the tone of such instruments he himself admitted that some of them did not sound well in the highest register. Recorders held their own until the middle of the eighteenth century, when they gave way to the cross flute. Today they survive only in the primitive forms of certain folk instruments, such as the *chakan* or *fayara*, or as a mere tone-maker, such as the signal whistle.

Because the bass recorder produced a tone with low volume and the handling of the double-bass pommer was very complicated, there arose a need for an instrument that would solve both these problems. The demands were met by the bassoon, whose invention is ascribed to the Italian Afranio degli Albonesi. His instrument, called the *fagotum*, does not, however, have much to do with the bassoon as we know it today. The origin of these instruments has not yet been sufficiently elucidated. Its German name Fagott appears for the first time in 1546 (W. H. Sallagar: *Die historische Entwicklung des Fagotts. Das Musikinstrument*, Frankfurt, 1959). It is also interesting that F. Behn believes that the Romans were responsible for its invention (*Musikleben im Altertum und frühen Mittelalter*, Stuttgart, 1954). Musical instruments from the Museum in Naples and the British Museum in London, upon which F. Behn bases his theory, are cross flutes with the side orifice placed in a small protuberance. The name of the first person to make a bassoon is not known, but he must have known the pommer, the bass recorder, the shawm and cromorne, and perhaps also the slide-trombone because he incorporated certain features of these instruments into his new invention, with the tube bent into the shape of the letter U. In the Renaissance period the bassoon was usually called the *dulcian*, and was characterized by two channels bored into a single piece of maple, cherry or pear-wood. These channels were connected by a cross bore and the holes stopped with a wooden plug. In addition to six tone-holes for the fingers of both hands and one key for the seventh tone-hole, the instrument had another two tone-holes and one key for both thumbs in the upper part of the channel. The dulcian had yet another interesting feature — a perforated lid covering the bell, which softened down the sound. Like other Renaissance musical instruments the

bassoon was also made in whole series. Praetorius speaks of eight bassoons — one descant instrument, two piccolo bassoons, three choir bassoons, one quarte and one quinte bassoon. The name 'choir bassoon' may be derived from the use of this instrument to support the bass in church choirs; this was for some time the main role of the bassoon. The modern bassoon is derived from this choir bassoon, whose fundamental scale was C major.

Half-way between wooden wind instruments, which they resembled in material and construction (wood, tone-holes), and the brasses, to which they belonged with their mouthpiece, come *zinks* or *cornetts*. As late as the eighteenth century German wind instrument orchestras were being named after them. In the eleventh century a distinction was already being made between the *straight cornett* and the *curved cornett*. The older one of the two is the straight cornett, which dates from the thirteenth century and had only five tone-holes and a bell made of animal horn. Later the straight cornett was made of one or more pieces of box-wood, the end of the tube was not flared, and the instrument had usually seven tone-holes, one on the back. The mouthpiece was made either of animal horn or of box-wood. It may have been made separately and thus gave the instrument a shriller sound, or was turned in one piece of the body. This latter type did not have

Tractate: Member of the Council

23

such a shrill sound and was therefore called the *mute cornett*. The straight cornetts referred to in the inventory lists of the Rožmberk orchestra as *Mundzink* and in the inventory of Archduke Charles as *Zingenmutti* are completely unknown to Mersenne. The curved cornett, whose flared bell was still seen in the sixteenth century, lived on until the beginning of the nineteenth century. Therefore, whenever there is a mention of the cornett in the eighteenth and nineteenth centuries it is always the curved cornett. Unlike the straight cornett it was made of two pieces of wood, usually walnut, which were glued together in the shape of a mildly curved crescent and covered with black leather.

The technique of play as well as the kind of embouchure are described by Daniel Speer (*Unterricht musikalischer Kunst*, Ulm, 1687). The embouchure was especially interesting and with high-pitched cornetts it differed much from the one used when playing brasses. The diameter of the mouthpiece of these cornetts usually did not exceed half an inch and therefore it was not possible to play it in the ordinary way. The mouthpiece was held between the lips and the sound produced without any pressure. This is the way instruments were played in ancient times, before the mouthpiece had been invented and when the tube was simply thrust into the mouth. Today we may find this interesting technique used for some folk instruments and high-pitched trumpets, such as the soprano E flat cornett or the Bach trumpet.

The sound of the cornett resembled that of the brasses, the high register the sound of trumpets, the lower register the sound of trombones. But it also possessed something of the timbre of the dulcian, especially when the instrument was played in high pitch. The wavering, groaning and uninteresting sound, in itself not pleasing to the ear but certainly very interesting in combination with other instruments, was last used by Gluck in his *Orpheus*.

The bass instrument among the cornett family was the *serpent*. Its tube was snake-shaped, so that the musician was able to reach all tone-holes. The serpent, too, was covered with black skin. It was used in churches and military bands, especially in France, until the middle of the nineteenth century, as the bass instrument of the trombone family.

The tone-holes of this instrument, which was in substance of the horn type, were not placed in the acoustically correct positions and therefore in unskilled hands the sound of the serpent was unstable and without the necessary brilliance. Today we regard with mixed feelings the enthusiasm of Mersenne, who declared that the serpent produced an excellent bass even in chamber music, without giving up decrescendo. Later, however, this enthusiasm faded. At the beginning of the nineteenth century some instrument-makers attempted to perfect the serpent by the introduction of keys. Rossini, Mendelssohn and Wagner composed some of their music for this kind of serpent. The Liverpool instrument-maker Jordan even des-

igned and made a double serpent, displayed at the London World Exhibition in 1851, but all attempts to rescue it were in vain, for it was replaced in the orchestra by instruments that had developed from it: first the bass horn and later the ophicleide and the bass tuba.

The doubled-up tube and the introduction of the slide paved the way for further development of brass instruments. A very important role in the development of the trombone was played by the slide trumpet. Illustrations of it may be found in numerous medieval works of art, the best-known of them being perhaps the altar triptych by Hans Memling in Antwerp. The musician held the instrument with one hand right at the mouthpiece, while the other operated the whole instrument. A later type of trumpet shared certain features with the trombone — the player firmly held the part of the tube with the bell and with his right hand moved the second part, which was in the shape of the letter U. When the size of the slide trumpet increased, all that had to be done was to change the principle of the operation of the slide and the trombone was invented. With the trombone — unlike the earlier type of slide trumpet — the player gripped with his left hand the tube with the bell, and with his right hand operated the U-shaped slide. The trombone is the only brass instrument that in the course of its development has not undergone any radical changes in its construction. The best-known trombone-makers were concentrated mainly in Nuremberg. The earliest name we know is that of Hans Neuschel, who lived at the end of the fifteenth century. He supplied his instruments to many orchestras owned by kings and the nobility, but not a single specimen has been preserved.

It is interesting that Renaissance stringed instruments do not show the diversity and ingenuity of construction of their wind counterparts. The variety of shapes seen in their medieval forerunners is reflected only in some minor changes in the shape of plucked instruments. But during the Renaissance the lute achieved widespread popularity and enjoyed a fame that — with the possible exception of the violin — exceeded that of any other musical instrument. The Renaissance raised the lute to the level of a work of art. The original pear-shaped body was given a new almond-like form and the edges were inlaid with ebony or ivory. The flat soundboard continued to be made of fine-grained spruce, but the rose covering the soundhole was decorated with beautiful Gothic designs. The number of strips of wood which were glued together to form the back was now increased, and they were often alternated with thin laminae of ebony or some other exotic wood. Carved ornamental designs were also applied to the low string-holder glued to the soundboard and to the large slanted peg-box.

Like all musical instruments in the Renaissance the lute developed into a whole family, ranging from the little octave lute to the bass lute, whose bass strings terminated in a special peg-box attached to an exten-

sion of the neck and were not parallel to the longitudi-
nal axis of the instrument. This line of development
led to the *theorbo lute, theorbo* and the *archlute* (or
chitarrone) with the neck reaching a length of more
than six feet. If we take into account the tremendous
popularity of the lute in the Renaissance period, it is
hardly surprising that the manufacture of lutes was
a very profitable enterprise up to the close of the
eighteenth century. The oldest lute-making centres
were the small town of Füssen on the frontier between
Bavaria and the Tyrol, and also Nuremberg. In the
sixteenth and the seventeenth centuries the centre
shifted to Italy, but Prague was by no means behind
the times. The *Liber contractuum* of 1571 mentions
a lute- and viol-maker by the name of Bartholomaeus
Markl, who worked at the court of Emperor Maxi-
milian II. And in Baron's book (*Untersuchung des
Instruments der Lauten*, Nuremberg, 1727) there is
praise for the Prague lute-maker Martin Schott
(1615—82). A beautiful *chitarra battente* in the collections of musical instruments at the Prague National
Museum is a testimony to his skill and artistry.

The lute, with its decoration of inlaid multicoloured
woods, tortoise-shell, ivory or mother-of-pearl, has
become a very attractive object for collectors. The
richest collection of lutes from the fifteenth and the
sixteenth centuries was in the famous Fugger Collection (*Kunstkammer*) in Augsburg, founded by
Raymund Fugger (1484—1535). Lutes made by such
outstanding instrument-makers as Laux Maler (called
the 'Stradivari of the lute', died in Bologna in 1528),
Hans Frey (father-in-law of Albrecht Dürer, died in
Nuremberg in 1523), Magnus Tieffenbrucker (died
in about 1625 in Venice) and many other masters of
their craft can be seen today at the Kunsthistorisches
Museum in Vienna. They come from the rich collection of the Ambras Castle in the Tyrol and from
the collections of Franz Ferdinand d'Este.

In the sixteenth century the fiddle developed a slim
neck with a scroll and frontal pegs, while the lyre family
was extended and now included a new bass member
with the Italian name *lirone perfetto*, which the musician played while standing. Both these stringed instruments paved the way for the appearance of the viol,
which combines the features and advantages of its
forerunners: arched soundboard with the soundholes
in the shape of the letter C, flat back, deep body, head
in the shape of a scroll and frontal pegs, narrow neck.
The viol, too, proliferated into a large family ranging
from the descant *viola da braccio*, through the tenor
viola da gamba to the double bass viol, an example
of which is kept at the Prague National Museum from
the orchestra of the Rožmberk family. These 'double
bass viols' were made in the second half of the sixteenth
century by Hans Vogel in Nuremberg (W. L. Lütgendorff: *Die Geigen- und Lautenmacher*, Frankfurt,
1922, II, p. 541). The viols became unchallenged masters of polyphonic music until the stringed instruments
of the violin family arrived on the scene. Their tone
was well balanced and they rendered the complexities

of counterpoint with surprising clarity. At the close
of the sixteenth century the *viola da braccio* gave rise
to the highest member of the family of stringed instruments — the *violin*, though its real fame was not to
come until later. Composers in the sixteenth century
did much to perfect and extend the renown of this
most important modern musical instrument. They
realized how lovely its sound was and they were also
quick to understand its suitability for orchestral performance. Thanks to them and to their initiative the
first outstanding instruments were made within a relatively short span of fifty to seventy years in the workshops of Duiffopruggar in Lyons and Gasparo da Salò
in Brescia.

During the Renaissance stringed instruments with
a keyboard appeared for the first time. In the fourteenth
century a psaltery-like instrument was equipped with
a keyboard and thus gave rise to the *clavichord*. The keys
of the clavichord are direct descendants of the bridges
of the monochord; they were attached to a rod terminating in tongues which struck and at the same time
stopped the string. By means of this simple mechanism
built into a narrow rectangular case, without registers
or pedals, it was possible to produce sounds of very
low volume. On the other hand the clavichord had the

A. Schlick:
Spiegel
der Orgelmacher
und Organisten

25

J. Aman:
Ehebrecherbrücke
des Königs Artus

advantage that a slight vibration of the hand could easily be transmitted to the string and thus the player was able to make minor changes in the pitch, which was naturally important. The German theorist Jakob Adlung wrote (*Musica Mechanica Organoedi*, Berlin, 1768, new edition Mahrenholz, 1931) that the clavichord had a nice tone of a low volume, and that no other instrument was better suited to playing ornaments. He also agrees with Johann Mattheson (*Das neueröffnete Orchester*, Hamburg, 1713, I, no. 3, chapter III, § 4) that thanks to its sweet and appealing sound the clavichord surpassed all other musical instruments.

Simultaneously with the clavichord, or perhaps a little later, there appeared another type of keyboard instrument, the strings of which were plucked with ravens' quills or leather tongues. This was one of various types of virginal, which differed in size, shape and the sophistication of their construction. In England and northern Europe the virginal was rectangular, while in Italy it was in the shape of an elongated pentagon. Very small virginals with a maximum compass of four octaves, the majority with only three or less, were called in Italy *ottavina* or *spinetta*, while in England they were given the name *octave virginals*, because they were tuned one octave higher than other virginals.

In the sixteenth century the keyboard was not parallel to the strings, but at right angles to them. This

particular arrangement gave rise to the *harpsichord*, which again had important advantages: greater compass and multiple strings. When the instrument was equipped with yet another keyboard it was possible to produce tones of new timbre. Various names were used for the harpsichord, such as *cembalo, gravicembalo, clavecin, clavicymbel, Flügel* and many others. The strings were plucked with a quill or a leather tongue and the tone, which was shriller than that of the clavichord, could be changed by means of manually operated registers. The harpsichord began to fall into disuse at the end of the eighteenth century, after almost three centuries of fluctuating popularity.

The delegation sent in 1457 by the Bohemian king Ladislav to the court of the French ruler Charles VII, to ask the hand of Princess Madeleine, brought many musical instruments, among them large kettle-drums. The cords keeping the membrane taut were replaced at the beginning of the sixteenth century by an iron band with several screws. The tympanists enjoyed the same rights as the trumpeters and their position in the orchestras of the nobility became firmly established. This most important membrane instrument of European orchestras was described by Sebastian Virdung (*Musica getutscht*, Basle, 1511) as 'gigantic and noisy casks. They are a pest to old and respectable people, the ill, the pious in the churches, who study, read and pray, and I firmly believe that they were invented by the Devil'.

Musicians in the orchestra of the Rožmberk family played these instruments in a most beautiful polyphonic style. Polyphony, which was a dominant feature of European music in the fifteenth and the sixteenth centuries and was introduced mainly by Dutch composers, was dependent upon well-trained orchestras. They included not only singers capable of performing very complex compositions in this style, but also instrumentalists who accompanied them. The singers in the orchestra of the Rožmberk family sang bass, tenor and falsetto alto. The descant part, on the other hand, was performed by Vavřinec Třeboňský and boy singers who stood before the music stand in such a manner that the older choristers could see the songbook over the heads of the others. The voices of the singers were amplified by musical instruments played by trumpeters and pipers. At the organ was the court organist and in the foreground, at the music stand, was the intoner who beat the time and indicated the pitch with his hand or a long baton. The orchestra amused the nobility at feasts by performing secular songs or instrumental arrangements called *carmina*. Musicians first arranged dance music for their instruments, but later they even used the 'Merry Songs' by Jeremias Hölzlin of Ambers, and jotted down on the title page of their score to 'sing or to play'. This increasing interest in instrumental music also had a far-reaching influence upon the development of musical instruments, though one that was quite different from that exerted by vocal music. In the Middle Ages instrumental music was a mere borrowing of vocal forms, but the instrumental style gradually refashioned the vocal style to suit its own needs and with it the musical instruments. The Rožmberk orchestra performed, in addition to the still predominant vocal style, compositions which show a certain tendency towards the instrumental style. It is true that the sudden development of the *a capella* style pushed instrumental music into the background for a time, but under Petr Vok, brother of Vilém of Rožmberk, this music was already firmly established. The *Ricercare* and *Cansona per sonar* are still an application of the vocal style to the instrumental one, but Demanti's 'Dances' represent an entirely new style, born of the special character of musical instruments.

The *Capella Dominorum de Rosis* performed the music on various occasions. One of the favoured forms was the 'table music', *musica pro tabula*, which engaged only a part of the orchestra. These were usually lute and viola da gamba players, who performed compositions with the double *canto firmo*, works based on the bass and tenor of the viola da gamba players, while the counterpoint descant, alto and the fifth part called *vagans* were plucked by the lute players. This arrangement of musical instruments was used mainly in the dining-hall and boudoirs of the castle, while on the terrace outside the musicians played pommers, windcap shawms and crumhorns. In moments of relaxation and quiet, especially after dinner, the musicians performed not only vocal music but also instrumental pieces. The intimate character of the music was also enhanced by the use of a group of the same instruments for example five or six windcap shawms, or the same number of pommers, crumhorns, recorders or viols.

The death of Petr Vok in 1611 spelt the end of the famous Rožmberk family, for he was its last member. It was also the end of the Rožmberk orchestra. Their precious musical archive was destroyed during the

Alta wind orchestra

wars with the Swedish armies, and from their rich collections of musical instruments only a few specimens have been preserved. The political situation following the Battle of the White Mountain in 1620 did not create the necessary climate for the further development of the European cultural stimuli that had animated the orchestra of the Rožmberk family. Consequently no important Czech musicians or composers emerged at that time. Only later, in the second half of the seventeenth century, did Czech musical life achieve any marked success, but this was under different political and cultural conditions.

CHOIRS AND CASTLES

Concert of sacred
music in the
Weimar church

At the close of the sixteenth century, a radical change
in the structure of music occurred. The polyphonic
style began to lose ground and a new style, monody,
took its place, in which the bass, called *basso continuo*,
became the most important element. Unlike the principle by which Renaissance music used the various
members of one family of instruments to create, in
accordance with polyphonic practice, a homogeneous
group of the same timbre, the basso continuo style
introduced a leading melody in one of the parts. This
new style attained a dominant position in an incredi-
bly short space of time, but did not involve any immediate and sweeping changes in the repertory of musical instruments. The individual instruments underwent some minor changes, so that they could meet the
requirements of new technique, timbre and melody.

At the beginning of the eighteenth century an
orchestra of instrumentalists played in the choir of
Weimar church, with the conductor reading the
organist's music and waving two short batons. A
period engraving from Walther's encyclopedia of
music gives a very good picture of this performance,
which was accompanied by the organ as a basso continuo instrument. After the Thirty Years' War the
Catholic Church used all possible means at its disposal
to revive its former glory. Beautiful churches were
constructed where liturgical singing was accompanied
by the organ. The positive, which in the Renaissance
period had two bellows and several registers, lived on
for some time, but was no longer able to meet the
increasing demands of pompous liturgy. Instrument-
makers began to build gigantic organs with a rich
variety of registers and several manuals. In the spirit
of *ars nova* the registers had various contrasting
timbres, while the Baroque style created for each
category of voices a special group of pipes, which
included virtually all sizes. Thus we can see that the
Renaissance period laid emphasis on the completeness
of the principal work, while Baroque organ-builders
were mainly concerned with the flute work. By means
of various combinations of these registers it was possible to create new kinds of timbre. The mechanism of
the organ was gradually perfected thanks to technical
and acoustic improvements, such as the invention of
air regulation and the introduction of temperament
tuning. The compass of the keyboard covered for
a long time C—C². A number of outstanding instrument-makers contributed to the art of organ-building,
among them the organ-builder and organist at the
Wolfenbüttel court, Esajas Compenius, who constructed the castle organ at Frederiksborg, Denmark,
Zacharias Hildebrand (c. 1690—1757); and Eugen
Casparini, predecessor of the famed Silbermann family
of organ-builders — Andreas (1712—83), who built

more than thirty organs in Basle, Kolmar, Strasbourg and other towns, and Gottfried (1683—1753), who is credited with the construction of forty-seven organs in Freiburg, Dresden, Zittau and elsewhere.

In another drawing we can see a concert of secular music conducted by Handel in London in about 1745 ('G. F. Handel with his musicians in London', from F. Volbach: *Das moderne Orchester in seiner Entwicklung*, Leipzig, 1910, plate III). Here the main basso continuo instrument is the harpsichord. (In Germany it was equipped sometimes with another set of strings with a sixteen-foot register. Thus the body of the instrument was much longer then before, but its tone was now very deep and rich.) The rather clattering chords of the harpsichord provided a harmonic framework for the polyphonic music, and the harpsichord player, guided by the movements of the first violinist's arms, directed the tempo by nodding his head. But we can see from this picture that Handel ranked higher than the harpsichord player and conducted the orchestra while standing, with a scroll of music in his hand. To attain greater volume of sound, two or even more harpsichords were used, which were accompanied by other basso continuo instruments, such as the harp, lute (the theorbo and chitarrone) and sometimes also by bass stringed instruments. In this case one of the harpsichord players accompanied the solos, while the others played *tutti*.

In seventeenth-century Italy the main group of musical instruments in the orchestra was made up of the stringed instruments, especially the violin. Violins made in the workshops of Cremona masters such as Nicola Amati (1596—1684), his disciple Antonio Stradivari (c. 1640—1737) and Giuseppe Guarneri (del Gesù, 1687—1742) are masterpieces of their kind. In their beauty, melodiousness and technical perfection no other instrument can be compared to them. It does not mean, however, that all violins have these qualities. Their tone may be more or less pleasant for the ear, depending upon the talent and skill of the maker. Violins made by the famous Italian masters of the seventeenth and the eighteenth centuries are outstanding and precious works of art, and may with justice be compared to paintings by Raphael or sculptures by Michelangelo.

Much as a blind person cannot comprehend colour, a man who has never heard such an instrument in the hands of a real artist cannot imagine the beauty of its tone. The sound of an Italian violin includes a whole mixture of timbres and may be likened to a costly perfume. We can hear in it the flute and the clarinet, as well as the soprano voice of a singer and many other undefinable timbres. Its effect upon the listener is therefore very complicated and defies definition. The violin family, too, includes many members, ranging from the violino piccolo, which was somewhat smaller than the violin and normally tuned a minor third higher, to the double bass violin, though the latter was often replaced by the double bass viol or violone. From the six-member violin family, first the piccolo

and the tenor violin sadly fell into disuse, and orchestral tenor parts today are shared by the viol and the violoncello. However the violoncello could not readily replace the viola da gamba, which played an important role in the history of improvisation, and held its own not only in music performed at home but also as a solo instrument. From the constructional point of view its deep body and flat back put it at a disadvantage compared to the violoncello, but the number of strings (five to six) and the special way of holding the bow (similar to the double bass in Germany) made it possible to play on three or even four strings simultaneously. Not until the end of the seventeenth century, when Stradivari designed the classical shape of the violoncello, did this instrument begin to take the place of viola da gamba.

For the first time in the history of musical instruments the varnish on the violin and its relatives began to play an important role. It not only protected the instrument from adverse environmental influences, such as humidity or changes in temperature, but also affected the quality of tone. It has the additional appeal of beauty, colour, translucency plus a quality that is very difficult to define and which we call in the case of precious stones 'play of light'. It is only natural therefore that the secret of the production and composition of varnish, which the Cremona masters had allegedly taken with them to the grave, has ever since presented a challenge not only to violin-makers but also to analytical chemists and even laymen.

In the orchestra the wind instruments were not contrasted with the stringed instruments, but played obbligato passages as solo instruments. To express sudden and violent contrasts it was necessary to increase the compass and dynamic flexibility of the instruments. In accordance with the demands of the new type of music, first to be dropped from the orchestra were all woodwind instruments with the windcap, such as the schryari, windcap shawms, crumhorns and later the cumbersome pommers and also sorduns and rankets. Of the woodwind instruments only three were retained — the shawms (*chalumeaux*), which developed in a very complicated process into the oboe, then the bassoon and finally the transverse flute. The flutes in the scores of Scarlatti, Lully, Bach and Handel are still recorders, not transverse flutes. The transverse flute was one of those rare wind instruments that existed in 'only' three sizes in the Renaissance. In the eighteenth century it became the most distinctive solo instrument. Of the brasses, the trumpets and trombones were retained without any major changes. The only newcomer in this group was the 'splendid pompous horn', as Mattheson called the instruments which makers developed from the hunting horn by lengthening the tube and decreasing the diameter of the body.

Two important instruments of the modern orchestra originated in the Baroque era — the clarinet and the piano. Johann Christoph Denner (1655—1707) cannot be regarded today as the only inventor of the clarinet.

91

XLV *Spinetta*

F. Bonanni:
Gabinetto armonico

conductor Faber. Johann Stamitz used it in his symphony 'avec clarinettes et cors de chasse', of 1755.

We do not know much more about the origin of another instrument, called at first the *gravicembalo col piano e forte*. The hammer action was known as early as in 1400, and in a manuscript in the Bibliothèque Nationale in Paris we can find a description of a cymbalo called *dulce melos*, which was equipped with a keyboard. It is also quite possible that the instrument mentioned by G. de Machault as *échequier* had a hammer action, because *échec* or *chec* means the same as 'a stroke'. Arnold Dolmetsch writes that he saw a piano dating from 1610, which was a whole century earlier than the first instruments made by Cristofori (Arnold Dolmetsch: *The Interpretation of the Music of the XVIIth and XVIIIth Centuries*, London, 1915, p. 431). It resembled a big cymbalo and had very small hammers attached to the keys in a manner used with the simple form of the Viennese action. One thing is certain, however: the invention of the piano had been in the air since the moment that musicians and composers alike realized the limited compass of the then existing keyboard instruments, the clavichord and the harpsichord. This may also explain the great success of Pantaleon Hebenstreit, who in 1705 presented in Paris a dulcimer of his own construction, which was named by King Louis XIV the *pantaléon*. The German organist and writer Gottfried Schröter (1699—1782) described in a letter how he had invented the hammer action in 1717, though he did not present two small-scale models of his instrument to the Dresden court until three years later (F. W. Marpurg: *Kritische Briefe über Tonkunst*, 1759—63, no. 139). In 1716, however, the Frenchman Jean Marius demonstrated before the Royal Academy in Paris models of an instrument made by him called a *clavecin à maillets*, which had a hammer action. But the Florence instrument-maker Bartolomeo Cristofori (1655—1736) constructed the first piano with hammers, in 1709. This fact is borne out by Adlung, who writes that Cristofori found a way to play forte and piano by means of hammers (*Anleitung zu der Musikalischen Gelehrtheit*, 1758, new edition Kassel, 1953).

The description in *Giornale dei letterati d'Italia* of 1711 makes it clear that the mechanism of Cristofori's instrument was in substance identical to the English action, because a hammer covered with buckskin struck the strings and a check prevented it from rebounding. Each key was also equipped with a separate damper. The first German maker of hammer pianos was the famous organ-builder Gottfried Silbermann, and from him the line of development goes directly to John Broadwood in England who constructed the modern English action in 1780.

The attempt to emphasize the individual character of musical instruments and to provide opportunity for solo performance had already led in the preceding century to a differentiation between chamber and orchestral effect. New instrumental forms appeared, both chamber and orchestral, which required changes

He did perfect the shawm, the development of which is considered by some scholars to be related to that of the oboe (W. Kleefeld: *Das Orchester der Hamburger Oper*, 1678—1738). To state the origin of the clarinet, its name and its first appearance in the orchestra is very difficult, because at first the clarinet shared the name with the shawm (*chalumeaux*). The word itself is derived from the Latin *clarinetto*, which is a diminutive of clarins, the register of a trumpet whose high-pitched tones were to recur in the clarinet. Denner's instrument had a small bell and seven tone-holes similar to the shawm, but the new additions were a single beating reed and two keys (one behind). The sound of clarinet in an orchestra was allegedly heard for the first time in 1720, in a mass by the Antwerp

in the construction of individual musical instruments and also in the composition of the orchestra. The stringed instruments were joined by the wind instruments, divided into woodwinds and brasses, and these completely replaced the plucked instruments. Up to this time the wind instruments had played the dominant role in the orchestra, but the new age decided in favour of the stringed instruments. In the estate of J. S. Bach were seventeen musical instruments which the great composer used to lend to music-lovers for a few months for a fee. It is interesting that there is not a single wind instrument among them. The importance of stringed instruments is also evident from the appearance of new types. The *viola da gamba* and the *lira da gamba* gave rise to the *viola bastarda*, which at the beginning of the seventeenth century had consonant strings but discarded them soon afterwards, in the second half of the century.

A combination of consonant strings with a plucking technique was used in the *viola di bardone*, also called the *baryton*, which in its size and tuning corresponded to the tenor gamba. In addition to the bowed strings running over the frets, the baryton had nine to twenty-seven consonant strings passing over a low bridge glued to the soundboard to a large peg-hole, which terminated in a carved male head with a cap. Like all other instruments of the gamba type the fingerboard of the baryton was equipped with frets. The consonant strings along the back of the neck were plucked with the thumb of the left hand. J. Maier derives the name baryton from the word 'pardon' (*Neu eröffneter theoretisch und praktischer Music-Saal*, 1741). His explanation is that a doctor under sentence of death saved his life by inventing the baryton and was later pardoned. The heyday of the baryton coincides with the activity of Joseph Haydn at the court of Nicholas Esterházy in the years 1765—75, when Haydn composed a number of pieces for it. The majority of instruments in museum collections come from the workshops of the Austrian violin-makers Daniel Achatius Stadlmann (c. 1680—1744) and his son Johann Joseph (1720—81), and also of Johann Blasius Weigert (1717—55), Magnus Feldtlen (seventeenth century) and Heinrich Kramer (second half of the seventeenth and early eighteenth century).

The best solution to the problem of the construction of consonant strings was achieved in the transformation of the *viola da braccio* into the *viola d'amore*. The consonant strings of the *viola d'amore* pass through the lower part of the bridge, along the neck, and are attached to the pegs in such a manner that they touch the body of the instrument as little as possible. The viola d'amore underwent many changes of shape; the soundholes were made in the form of small flames. The instrument is somewhat bigger than the violin, has a deeper body and a flat back which slants gently towards the neck. The long peg-box with a great number of pegs is often decorated with the winged head of an angel or the putti with bound eyes. The *viola d'amore* was a rather difficult instrument to play, for its

XLVII *Arcileuto*

strings had to be retuned often, sometimes by great intervals. But the compass exceeded that of the violin by nearly an octave, its lowest string being usually around the pitch of the viola. It is true that the playing technique was more difficult than for other stringed instruments, but this drawback was compensated by its peculiar and melodious sound, which was described by Berlioz as angelic, combining something of the sound of viol and the high-position harmonic tones of the violin. Like the majority of other viols, whose number of strings and mildly arched bridge made it possible to play chords of four or even more tones, the viola d'amore was at first used to accompany singing. Later, however, it became one of the most

F. Bonanni:
Gabinetto armonico

31

favoured solo instruments of the eighteenth century. When a seventh string was added it proved more of a drawback than an advantage, because it was such a strain upon the soundboard that the already low-volume sound was further weakened. The close of the eighteenth century witnessed an attempt to increase the volume of the sound of musical instruments and consequently the viola d'amore, with its pleasant but low-volume sound, quickly lost ground. The composers of the romantic era tried to enhance the intimacy and lyrical character of their works and therefore used anew the viola d'amore, for example in Meyerbeer's opera *The Huguenots*. But this come-back was of only short duration.

Side by side with the current types of stringed instruments appeared various related types, but they did not have the necessary vitality to survive for a longer period of time. Thanks to J. S. Bach, a five-stringed *viola pomposa* was constructed in Germany, and in France there appeared a kind of five-stringed gamba called the *quinton*. The *basso di camera* had the same number of strings or even more, and in the middle of the eighteenth century a descant viol called the *pardessus de viole* was invented.

FROM CASTLE SALONS TO CONCERT HALL

While in the Baroque period music had a universal character, the nineteenth century witnessed a wave of national movements. The little salons of the nobility were replaced after the French Revolution by the concert-halls of the rising bourgeoisie. This was an era of travelling virtuosos, whose lives were often shrouded in many legends. The Genoa-born Niccolo Paganini performed such acrobatics on his violin that he was often believed to be a magician. Franz Liszt, who displayed unbelievable audacity and drive at the keyboard of his piano, brought storms of admiration from his audience that can hardly be imagined today. The demands made on musical instruments, both in terms of technique and sound, were steadily increasing. Therefore violins made by Antonio Stradivari and Guarneri del Gesù, with their clear tones, were preferred to those built by Jacob Stainer, with arched soundbox and a weak, flute-like sound. The mechanism of the hammer piano, whose sound was still dull and weak, was improved in many ways. In the last quarter of the eighteenth century the 'Viennese action' was invented and almost simultaneously with it the 'English action'. At the Paris World Exhibition in 1823 Erard presented to the public his double escapement (*double échappement*). At the same time Streicher constructed in Austria a hammer mechanism that struck the strings from above; this was the start of a development which led to the mechanism of the upright piano.

The progress of industry brought in its wake many improvements in the manufacturing technique for musical instruments. Factory production gradually replaced small workshops. The mounting popularity of brass instruments resulted in the formation of the first popular bands, whose composition and technique of performance often followed the example of military bands. The true beauty and romantic value of wind instruments were revealed by Carl Maria von Weber in his opera *Der Freischütz*. They were further developed by Berlioz, who provided a third player for the woodwinds: the piccolo for the flutes, the cor anglais for the oboes, and the bass clarinet for the clarinets as well as the contra bassoon for the bassoons. Wieprecht and Moritz were building tubas in the 1830s, and in Paris Adolf Sax invented the *saxophone* for the French army. This endeavour to create new sound effects is reminiscent of the Renaissance period, it is true, but the underlying purpose is not so much polyphonic contrast and clarity as greater emotional impact. The demand for expressive and emotional music gave to the growing orchestra new instruments and multiplied them in numerous registers. Clarinets were made in at least twelve sizes and saxophones in five. In order to meet all the demands of the composer, who now planned the orchestration of his piece down to the smallest detail, it was necessary to make some sweeping changes in the family of wind instruments. The simple trumpet, for example, was fitted with keys or stops like woodwinds by Weidinger in Vienna in 1801, and twelve years later Blühmel and Stölzel invented the modern valve trumpet, which became the leading descant instrument among the basses. A similar development may be observed when we study the history of the French horn. The key mechanism of the woodwind instruments was improved and the number of keys steadily increased. After many attempts French instrument-makers designed a system of stops with ring-keys for the oboe — this was about the year 1840 — and for the flute and clarinet Boehm's system was introduced. The harp, which was established by Berlioz as a permanent member of the symphonic orchestra, became chromatic after thousands of years of development, and the kettle-drums, whose tuning had always caused considerable difficulty, were now easily tuned by means of pedals.

The revolutionary change in music, with its centres in Mannheim, Paris and Vienna, was mainly a question of individualizing the various instrument groups as well as the instruments themselves.

In order to attain greater perfection of playing technique as well as of mode of expression, Mannheim composers of Czech extraction proceeded to reform the Mannheim orchestra and its whole structure. The creation of a new dynamic scale laid the foundations of the laws of balance of the modern orchestra. The first far-reaching consequences of the reforms initiated by the Mannheim and pre-classical masters may be seen in the work of Gluck, Haydn and Mozart. We may say with justice that in their hands balance was finally established between the wind and the stringed instruments, their individual roles and their place in the orchestra, the intensity of their timbres and their individual and combined possibilities. At the end of the eighteenth century the orchestra experienced its first classical period, as if it were a single musical instrument, or the most perfect of all musical instruments, demanding from the composer independent orchestral thinking. In the nineteenth century the composers of operas and symphonies extended the orchestra to gigantic proportions. The number of strings was increased compared to the times of Spohr and Habeneck, but soon the wind instruments followed suit. The mammoth orchestra for Berlioz's *Requiem* was unequalled throughout the nineteenth

century, but Wagner began to limit the number of instruments he used.

At first glance it may seem that our century has taken over the instruments of the Romantic period unchanged. This is not altogether true, though Richard Strauss's contributions are drawn from Berlioz's theory of instrumentation. Strauss's smaller orchestra for his opera *Salome* included the following instruments: piccolo, four flutes, two oboes, English horn, heckelphone, five clarinets, bass clarinet, three bassoons, double bassoon, four trumpets, six French horns, four slide trombones, bass tuba, four kettle-drums, small kettle, tom-tom, cymbals, large and small drum, tambourine, triangle, xylophone, castanets, chimes, two harps, celesta, thirty-two violins, ten to twelve violas, ten violoncellos, eight double basses. Off stage were harmonium and organ. Seven years later, in 1912, his *Ariadne auf Naxos* had more solo parts, with a predominance of instruments on which chords can be played. Particularly remarkable is the chamber division of the strings: two flutes, two oboes, two clarinets, two bassoons, two French horns, one trumpet, trombone, celesta, harmonium, two harps, piano, six violins (three stands), four violas (two desks), four violoncellos (two stands), and two double basses. The return of the piano into the orchestra, and the chamber orchestration with its emphasis on wind instruments, seemingly point to a new direction in music, but in fact are only a continuation of nineteenth-century tendencies. The same is true of the percussion instruments. In Stravinsky's *L'Histoire du Soldat* there are

B. Picart:
Violoncello player

33

six melodic instruments with the same number of percussion instruments. This development is understandable if we take into account the fact that for centuries harmony had been superseded by rhythm. It would not be surprising, therefore, if twentieth-century music fell back upon the structure of the rhythm, just as the seventeenth century based its music upon the basso continuo.

Occasionally featuring in the modern orchestra are the *heckelphone*, *dulcimer* and *saxophone*. The composition of the orchestra, as well as the use of some instruments, are of course highly individual matters, determined by the composition itself. Various theories dealing with orchestration are thus only the bare framework for the great possibilities of orchestral colouring. The inexhaustible wealth of orchestral sound makes itself felt only in practice. In conclusion we may say that the development of musical instruments and the numerous improvements made to them ran parallel to the increasing demands and were closely bound up with them, until they culminated in the maximum of sound effect found in the modern orchestra. All this could not have been achieved without the unceasing efforts of the human mind. The final result of the whole process is the incomparably beautifu sound of the modern orchestra as we know it today

THE WORLD OF JAZZ INSTRUMENTS

At the beginning of this century the specific conditions in the United States of America gave rise to a kind of music which has features typical of African musical culture, as well as of European music. The African features include responsorial or antiphonal technique, heterophony, based upon melodic modifications, and above all, typically Negro interpretation: glissando, vibrato, neutral and guttural tones. Among the European features we find basic harmonic functions and some influences in instrumentation. This kind of music, called jazz, has undergone a number of changes during its short life and has occupied an important position in the life of modern man.

Like all other kinds of music, jazz has its own world of musical instruments. These are basically the acoustic instruments of European music, but they are played in a different style and sometimes with a different technique. This specific technique is the result of many influences, but the most important is the adoption of the intonation of Negro folk-songs in instrumental music. While the classical musical instruments require discipline and meticulous observance of the score, jazz instruments call for the greatest possible independence, imagination and flexibility. In performing classical music the musician tries to give expression to the composer's intentions, while the jazz musician improvizes and strives to master the technique of his instrument, so that he may be able to realize in the best possible way the ideas he gets while playing. The primary role of a jazz musical instrument is to 'speak'. Thus its tone is not used only for its beauty, clarity and perfection, but also for its capacity to engender emotions that had often been neglected by other kinds of music. This is the reason why jazz instruments produce some unusual and certainly not pleasing sounds, such as alarm glissando, vibrato, tremolo, as well as tones of indescribable timbre.

The theory of jazz divides musical instruments into two categories — melodic and rhythmic. The first category includes all non-percussion instruments, while the percussion instruments, the piano and the double bass come into the second one. At first glance the classification of the piano and the double bass seems to be illogical. For a long time jazz music had only contempt for the melodic qualities of the piano, but in the end it was accepted into the family of jazz instruments, though it was given the role of a rhythmic instrument. In an orchestra without percussion the double bass has an important rhythmic function.

The history of jazz may be traced according to the ups and downs of individual instruments. In the early history of jazz stands the piano, which was the leading instrument of the ragtime period. This is instrumental music, especially piano music, characterized by strong syncopation. Ragtime is important for the birth of jazz, though it differs from its early forms in that it is composed music. The leading role was now taken over by the trumpet and the clarinet. The swing era — a jazz style of the thirties, which represents the transition from classical to modern jazz — was a period of saxophones. Jazz music can be played on virtually any musical instrument, which may be why no established or stereotyped composition for the jazz band has ever appeared. But jazz music 'discovered' some musical instruments that had never been used in it before. The speed with which the flute, in a relatively short time, became one of the established jazz instruments is an instructive example. It seems that the French horn may be on its way to a similar development. All recent changes in the family of jazz instruments seem to argue for a more frequent use of the strings, despite the fact that the violin has always been considered too delicate for jazz music.

In its early development jazz music even resorted to some improvized instruments, such as the washboard, which was played by rhythmic movements of the fingers, sticks, or even thimbles. The washboard was used in various jazz bands and for a short period round 1950 it was even popular in Europe. Another instrument important for the rhythm was the washtub, which was turned upside down. A broom-stick or a pole was fixed upright to the washtub bottom and between the bottom and the top end of the pole were strung strands of horse-hair or a cord, which were plucked, bowed or struck. Among the very important and much favoured members of the early jazz bands were also various kinds of *mirlitons*. These are instruments which change the human voice into nasal sounds and their shape is very often modelled upon wind instruments. Often they are just a tube (reed, a piece of water pipe) with one end stopped with a paper membrane into which the player sings or hums. This instrument, called the *kazoo*, was a substitute for the trumpet in popular jazz bands. A similar device was the narrow-mouthed jug (or bottle) into which the musician blew or hummed rhythmically.

In a later stage of the development of jazz, new instruments began to appear in the bands or orchestras. They include for instance the *banjo*, originally a simple stringed instrument with the soundbox made of a gourd or coconut shell, but later a typical jazz instrument. The banjo was used in early 'processional' jazz bands. The banjo took over the function of the alto horn and the bugle in the middle passages, but it also strengthened the percussive rhythm. The musician had to play chords on it, for this was the only way it could replace the harmony of its predecessors and hold its own against the wind instruments. The technique of solo play — and this is true also of the guitar — came into its own later, at the end of the classical period of jazz and under the influence of the blues — a vocal form of Afro-American music which exerted considerable influence upon the development of jazz. It found its expression in be-bop — a style which originated in the forties as a reaction to swing. Its characteristic feature is the irregular rhythm of the melody. Modern bands prefer the guitar, which first replaced the banjo as an instrument on which chords are played and later usurped its solo function. At first the guitar was played by plucking the strings with the fingers or nails in the European fashion. But later guitar players took over from popular music a new technique — the strings are played with several fingers at once. Under the influence of the original percussive character of banjo play there developed from the European concert guitar what is known as the gibson, which is somewhat larger and more sturdily built than the ordinary guitar. It has an arched soundboard with the soundholes in the shape of the letter F (as with the violin) or the letter C (as with the gamba). Its

V. Hollar:
Joyful Music

strings are metallic and this is a definite advantage, for it can now hold its own against the wind instruments. The fourteen frets on the neck make it quite easy to play high-pitched notes, as high as b^2. It is a typical feature of the gibson that the chords are played with a plectrum on all strings, the musician using a special technique of fingering called *barrée* — the index finger touches all strings and thus has the role of an additional fret.

Some jazz bands incorporated the violin of ragtime orchestras, but its position was very difficult, because the winds naturally have a sound of much higher volume. Also, the violin is incapable of 'hot' intonation, which is characterized by strong rhythms and free melodic improvization, and it therefore does not occupy an important position in the repertory of jazz musical instruments. The situation is different, however, when we study the history of the double bass. In the jazz bands of the past the role of the double bass used to be taken by the tuba or the sousaphone. Both these bass brass instruments came to the jazz orchestra from military bands, but in the swing era they were gradually replaced by the double bass. Those instruments that are made specially for jazz bands sometimes have an arched back, and the body is modelled on the shape of the violin, which makes it easier for the musician to play high tones. It is not known exactly when the bow was replaced by the pizzicato technique. The story of a New Orleans double bass player who broke his bow and had to pluck the strings of his instrument throughout the evening performance is very probably apocryphal, but it is true that in New Orleans the double bass had a very strong competitor in the tuba. The tradition of the latter instrument was so strong that as late as the thirties double bass players could play the tuba as well. At first the strings were played with the bow, but now almost all musicians use the pizzicato technique, plucking the strings with their right index finger. But it is advantageous to use the index finger and the middle finger alternately. The fundamental rhythm of modern jazz is based upon four crotchets to a bar, and here the pizzicato technique fulfils its rhythmic function much better than the tuba. But the double bass can also be played as a solo instrument and in this case the musician certainly has the same possibilities of improvization as the rest of the orchestra.

That the piano did not play a more important role in the birth of jazz was due mainly to purely technical difficulties. But as early as 1910 the piano had two tasks in jazz music: it fulfilled the function of percussion instrument and also played the melody, especially in the blues, which, together with dances, were an important part of the repertory. In comparison with other instruments, the piano has a number of advantages in jazz music. In addition to monophony and polyphony, the player can create rhythm on it and even harmonize, as can the double bass, but this is further combined with a wide range of possibilities in the sphere of melody. No other instrument gives the musician such possibilities of expressing his own talent and artistry. It is in fact a whole orchestra combined in one instrument. In small rooms jazz musicians used to play on the upright piano, and in the first three decades of this century a mechanical piano called the *pianola* or *phonola* was quite popular in the United States of America; ragtime indeed owes much of its popularity to it. The piano became a typical instrument in solo music, accompaniment as well as orchestras. This ability to play both melody and rhythm gave rise to a number of very interesting techniques. Some of them were born of the assimilation of European techniques, while others are applications of banjo or guitar play. The piano technique naturally developed in relation to the repertory. Piano ragtime was taken over by the whole orchestra and the piano itself played a leading role. The same is true of the blues, which entered classical jazz music not only in its vocal form but in both instrumental forms as well — the barrel-house style (mainly in city saloons of the north) and boogie-woogie style. The latter is an early piano interpretation of the blues and was later taken over by other instruments of the orchestra. It is characterized by a persistent rhythmic bass. The blues brought with them their own technique, which doubled the guitar and the bass beat — the fundamental rhythmic stress of jazz music played by the rhythmic section or perceived subconsciously. This one-tone technique is called the jazz-band piano style. In the course of further development piano players gradually transfer-red the beat and bass functions to the cymbals and the double bass. The rhythmic function of the piano was roughly identical with that of the small drum, which interrupted the continuous rhythm of the cymbals and of the high-hat (cymbals with pedals) with their syncopated off-beats. The off-beats give jazz music its typical rhythmic tension. As a member of the rhythm section the pianist contented himself with playing individual off-beat chords now and then and thus indicated chord sequences. Early jazz pianists rarely used the right pedal, and the piano, with its shrill tone, was always a percussion instrument, even when it occasionally played melody.

Under the influence of European romantic and impressionistic music jazz piano technique adopted diffuse pedal timbres, while in snobbish jazz (as opposed to commercial jazz music) — which tries to be different, unconventional and uncommercial at any cost — many pianists fell back upon the old percussion technique and produced clear hard tones. To make the picture complete we must also mention the fact that the harp has its own jazz history in the sphere of blues music. But chord alterations, so typical of modern jazz, cannot be played on the harp without complicated tuning.

Among wind instruments the saxophone is an indispensable member of the jazz orchestra. Thanks to its excellent sound and technical qualities it became an ideal jazz instrument, surpassed only by the trumpet, with its clear and characteristic sound, and the technically flexible clarinet. Jazz music took over the saxophone from American brass bands, where it is still an indispensable instrument today. But it has never been suited to hot intonation, for its technical qualities do not permit this. It is true that hot intonation is sometimes played on it, but then the instrument is forced to fulfil a function which is not natural to it.

It is interesting to note that the saxophone is not an original jazz instrument. It was invented, as already mentioned, in the middle of the last century by the Belgian instrument-maker Adolph Sax, whose intention was to enhance the richness of tone of woodwind instruments in the symphonic orchestra. Only very few people are aware of the fact that jazz saxophones differ from those used in the symphonic orchestra in one slight detail — the shape of the mouthpiece, which makes shriller intonation possible on jazz saxophones. Of the numerous members of the saxophone family jazz music adopted first the soprano saxophone, which replaced the clarinet. Shortly afterwards jazz orchestras accepted the alto saxophone as well as the tenor saxophone, then came the bass and lastly the baritone saxophone. In swing and modern jazz, saxophones play an increasingly important role not only as big-band instruments — big band includes four trumpets, four trombones, five saxophones, and the rhythmic section made up of piano, double bass and percussion — but also as solo instruments, gradually replacing the clarinets and trombones that had once been so important. They have a wide range of technical possibilities

Music at the court
of a Bavarian
nobleman

and a rich tone — sonorous in the low register, rather tender in the middle register and relatively shrill in the high register. The most frequently used is certainly the tenor saxophone, whose development took a course entirely different from that of the clarinet. While the clarinet in jazz orchestras was gradually losing its popularity, the tenor saxophone reached dizzy heights of fame. In the beginning it was played by only a handful of musicians, including Coleman Hawkins, but at present their numbers are tremendous. Of the woodwinds the clarinet occupies a leading position in jazz music, which is characterized by its intermediary role between the trumpet and the trombone. Much less favoured are the flute, the oboe and the bass clarinet. The bassoon is rarely used in jazz music.

The trumpet, on the other hand, is often called the 'royal instrument of jazz'. Unlike the trumpet in the symphonic orchestra, the jazz trumpet has a narrower bore and is always equipped with piston valves (whereas in Germany and central Europe the orchestral trumpet has rotary valves). But before the arrival of the trumpet on the jazz scene in the 1930s, jazz orchestras used the cornet, an instrument that resembles the trumpet but has a weaker tone. It is also shorter than the trumpet; its funnel-shaped bell is wider and the mouthpiece is not so shallow. After the First World War the fundamental character of jazz music underwent some sweeping changes and these brought in their wake a replacement of the cornet by the trumpet, which offered a richer tone and made it possible for

musicians to display their bravura technique. Jazz musicians are fond of the stimulating effects of the high-pitched tones of their instrument, which are beyond the ordinary compass of the trumpet. Californian musicians representing the west coast style — also called the 'Californian style', it originated in the fifties along the western coast of the United States of America and is close to European music — introduced into their orchestras the bass trumpet and the French horn.

Apart from the trumpet, the most important mouthpiece instrument in jazz is the slide trombone. Its history is very old, though at first it was simply a substitute for the double bass and provided the fundamental harmony for improvizations with trumpet and clarinet. The technique for playing the slide trombone in jazz is very similar to that of the trumpet, but the slide also makes it possible to use Negro vocal intonation, not only in very impressive glissandos but also in arbitrary intonation. In big bands trumpets and trombones are included in the brass section, as opposed to the reed section — saxophones. In the old brass bands of New Orleans the trombone supplied the bass, while the style used by the first important jazz trombone player, Kid Ory, already represented an advanced stage of development. It was called the tail gate, and this name is explained by the fact that the trombone player needs more room than other musicians. On the wagons taking jazz bands through New Orleans streets the trombone player sat or stood at the rear where he could find sufficient room to play his

37

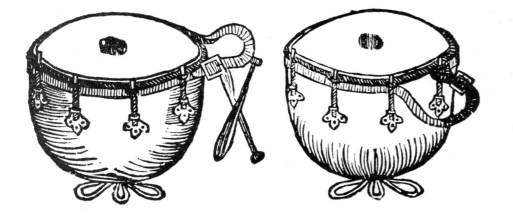

instrument comfortably, for the slide reached over the side, making it possible for him to play impressive glissando cadences.

A characteristic feature of mouthpiece instruments is the use of various mutes which can change the tone into grotesque sounds. At first the musicians were content to use anything, even a hat, that could be held close to the bell of the instrument. Later, however, two fundamental types of mutes were developed: conical mutes, which make the tone shrill, and pear-shaped ones producing a nasal timbre (these have various names, such as straight mute, hush-hush, wow-wow and many others).

Idiophones and membrane musical instruments are classed with the percussion group, irrespective of their melodic or rhythmic function. The *vibraphone* does not differ much from its immediate forerunner, the *marimba*. Instead of wooden bars and resonators it is equipped with metal ones. Its name is derived from the vibrating tone produced in motor-driven resonators. The tone-producing technique, however, is not of a jazz character, and the vibraphone was therefore only very slowly established in jazz music.

From the very beginnings of jazz the percussion instruments were the keepers of rhythm. They include the bass drum with two heads, which is today about half the size of the original instrument. Attached to the bass drum was the side drum, but at present it is placed next to the bass drum on its own stand. During the swing era among the new requisites of the drummer appeared fan-shaped wire brushes with which the musician produced delicate rattling sounds on the side drum or the cymbals, and the metal handle of the wire brush may occasionally be struck against the cymbal. The percussion instruments also include saucer-shaped idiophones made of zinc/copper and called cymbals. They used to be played in pairs, but today we find them either attached to a special rod in twos and played by means of a pedal (high-hat), or played individually and struck with drum sticks. The beat function of the side as well as the bass drums is transferred in modern jazz to the cymbals and occasionally to the high-hat. Similar effects to those produced on the high-hat may also be played on the Charleston cymbal, a pair of cymbals operated with a pedal. The rhythmically articulated beat in be-bop is produced on suspended cymbals.

In addition to these instruments, the percussion section sometimes included various auxiliary instruments such as the *timpani*, which in jazz are called the *timbals* — these lack the hollow brass or copper hemisphere. In this group come the two-headed *tom-toms*, small longish blocks of wood with a long slit along the narrow side called *wood-blocks*, and similar hollow balls made of wood and with an oval hole called *temple blocks*. *Cow-bells* resemble the object from which their name is derived, but they lack the clapper, and were attached individually or in groups to the bass drum. After the Second World War all these instruments went out of fashion and the percussion section adopted new ones, this time from the Afro-Cuban repertory. Among them we find the one-headed kettle-shaped drums called the *conga*, *tumba* and *bongo*, the *claves*, which are pairs of wooden sticks, rattles called *maracas* and the scraper known under the name of *güiro*. In the course of time even the function of percussion instruments changed. Today they are not only rhythmic instruments but may also fulfil a melodic function. This does not mean, however, that they have given up their original rhythmic purpose. Jazz musicians today take a more complex view of their rhythmic function, and this fact may explain why they are often assigned a melodic role.

ELECTRIC MUSICAL INSTRUMENTS

The development of musical instruments has always been closely bound up with technical progress. The complicated mechanism of the organ or mechanical musical instruments, harps, the keys of woodwinds and the system of levers controlling the valves of brass instruments are good examples of this phenomenon. But alongside this technical development and improvement, many philosophers, theoreticians and scholars pursued another course — they were less interested in the musical instruments as such and paid much more attention to natural phenomena and the way they were interrelated. This also led them to study acoustics. The resulting symbiosis of sound-waves and electricity gave rise to electric musical instruments, which in their turn caused far-reaching and revolutionary changes in the development of music, the consequences of which are still a matter of conjecture today. Musicians, who are often described as a conservative element bitterly opposed to any innovations, regard such modern musical instruments as a betrayal of sacred traditions, as conceited decadence and arrogant iconoclasm. But such opinions are born largely of insufficient knowledge of the construction of these instruments, which is based upon advanced technology and which is for the layman only a maze of wires, levers, capacitors and many more things known only to the electrical engineer. A better understanding of eletrical musical instruments is also impeded by the fact that many musicians identify them with extremist movements in music, with electronic or even twelve-tone music. Today, after about a century of development in electric musical instruments, conditions seem to have much improved, because musicians are becoming aware of the significance and consequences of this revolution in music, which is opening up for all of us a new and hitherto unknown world of sounds.

Electric musical instruments are the fulfilment of the daring plans and dreams of many scholars and inventors in the past, which are mentioned in their treatises by the medieval theorists of music Baryphon and Calvisius and by Mersenne in the seventeenth century. These instruments realize the age-old desire of mankind to preserve sound and reproduce it again as faithfully as possible, to create musical instruments that can produce an unlimited number of timbres. The oscillation of electric current changed into sound-waves makes this possible and thus creates an entirely new system of sounds, independent of the classical musical instruments, and also its own world of electric musical instruments.

Attempts to use electricity in the construction of musical instruments go back to the first half of the eighteenth century. At that time the Czech-born inventor of a lightning conductor, Prokop Diviš, attrac-ted considerable attention not only at home but also abroad with his electric orchestrion called *Denis d'or*. Thirty years later the Frenchman La Borde announced his own invention of the 'electric piano'. But all these attempts at using electricity in the creation of sound were limited to very modest ones to cause the vibration of some flexible material by means of electricity. It took a number of scholars and inventors many years to replace the complex acoustic phenomena, which are very difficult to control, with those of the electricity. The decisive turning-point in the development of electric musical instruments was the discovery by Heinrich Hertz of the existence of electromagnetic waves.

The first musical instrument with tones produced by electricity was constructed by the American Tadeus Cahill in 1895. If we take into account that the inventor used ordinary telephone earphones as the loudspeaker, we must consider his instrument as an example of praiseworthy endeavour, rather than a real musical instrument. Still, it did enjoy considerable popularity among the public. However, these first promising steps did not at first lead to any positive results, because electricity as a new element in music could not fight the existing musical traditionalism with the weapons it had at its disposal. Many more new ideas and inventions and much better quality of sound were needed before musicians began to take a more favourable view of these new musical instruments. These came, however, as late as after the First World War.

Electric musical instruments, with their whole new world of sounds and aspirations, sounded for the first time before the public in 1921—27. They may be divided into two groups, according to their construction. The first included instruments based upon the interference of two high-frequency (that is inaudible) alternating currents, the 'radio whistle'. This is a very unpleasant problem with old radio sets, but now this whistle could be reproduced and its intensity, timbre and acuity, as well as duration, intentionally controlled by a generator. The alternating current with the frequency one million and one million and sixteen cycles per second produced in the loudspeaker a differential tone of sixteen cycles per second, which means subcontra C. By increasing one of the frequencies it was possible to produce higher tones, and their timbre could be changed by partial tones. The most popular instrument of this group was the *tereminvox* constructed by the Soviet physicist Leonid Teremin. In the case of this instrument one of the high-frequency signals had a constant frequency, while the other was tuned by the capacity of the hand, namely by approaching the hand to an iron rod sticking out of the instrument. With one hand the musician changed the colour of the sound while he waved the other in the air, as if drawing the tones from the ether. These curious gestures are responsible for some historical names for electronic music in general — 'ethereal music', 'music of the air' or even 'music of the spheres'. The tereminvox was favourably received by the public and A. F. Pashchenko even composed an orchestral piece for this instrument, his *Symphonic Mystery*, which was first played in Leningrad in 1924.

The second group of electric musical instruments worked with an alternating current of the frequency of sixteen to twenty thousand cycles per second. Among them we may mention Bertrand's *dinaphone*, which had two valves and a rotary capacitor.

After the initial success many more electric musical instruments were constructed in the thirties. The monophonic electric keyboard instrument known today all over the world as *Martenot's waves* (les ondes Martenot) has outlived all its contemporaries and is still widely used. Its inventor, the Frenchman Maurice Martenot, even introduced teaching of the playing of this instrument at the Paris Academy of Music. The audience heard it for the first time at the Paris Opera in 1928. Among the artists who composed or still compose for Martenot's waves are such outstanding names as Olivier Messaien, Darius Milhaud, André Jolivet, Jacques Ibert and many others. Arthur Honegger, who used Martenot's waves in his *Joan of Arc*, characterized its diversity of tones in these words: 'The instrument becomes a Panpipe, a roaring monster, the sound of natural elements, or the voice of the heavens. No other musical instrument offers such a wide range of possibilities, such a complete scale of sounds ranging from the lowest to the highest, from those that resemble noise to those that are true musical tones. The instrument is now capable of harmony as well as monophony'.

The inventor of the quarter-tone reed-organ, the German teacher, mechanic and organist Jörg Mager, also constructed the *spherophone* and the 'electric organ'. The most important improvement and innovation of Mager's 'organ', which is the first really significant application of electro-acoustic phenomena in music, is not only the glissando effect but also the creation of innumerable timbres. Mager is also credited with the invention of other electric musical instruments, particularly the *kaleidophone*, which is a combination of three spherophones, the *electrophone* and the *partiturophone*.

All these instruments inspired a professor at the Leningrad Academy of Music, G. M. Rimski-Korsakov, grandson of the famous Nikolai Rimski-Korsakov, to construct his *emiriton* in 1930. His octet for two emiritons, three brasses and three strings was composed in 1932. A professor of acoustics at the Berlin Hochschule für Musik, Friedrich Trautwein, achieved considerable success with his low-frequency *trautonium*. It was originally a monophonic instrument, but was later improved so that it was possible to play four

voice parts on it. Among the composers whose works were intended for this instrument are Paul Hindemith, Richard Strauss and many others. Like the instruments made by Jörg Mager and Rimski-Korsakov, the trautonium made glissandos and a wide range of sound timbres possible. But Mager and Rimski-Korsakov worked with musical sounds only, while Trautwein used all kinds of sound and even those that occur in human speech. Thus, it was possible to 'play' on the trautonium various vowels and consonants, which gave the impression of human or animal voices.

In addition to the electric musical instruments already mentioned, there appeared between the two world wars other instruments using the selenophone (Spielman's *superpiano*) or based upon a combination of the mechanical and electric creation of sound. Shortly before the Second World War the Telefunken Company constructed a monophonic musical instrument by combining two different electric musical instruments. But all existing instruments had one very serious shortcoming — they were very difficult to handle and made very great demands upon the hearing and the musical awareness of the performer.

During the Second World War the development of electric musical instruments came to a standstill, but immediately after the end of the war their production made quick progress. New and much better types than before appeared, and the handling of them was much easier thanks to the keyboard. The manufacturers of electric musical instruments at present use one of these three systems: the first is based upon the synthesis of harmonic waves, the second uses what is known as the formant theory and is particularly suited to the imitation of classical musical instruments, and finally the third system is based upon tone-generators that give the desired wave-form.

In practice the term 'electric musical instruments' is applied to all musical instruments whose tone is either created or modified electrically. They are divided in the following manner:

I Electro-acoustic musical instruments. These are based upon mechanical vibrations which are picked up and transformed into electric current. This group includes either classical instruments, such as guitars and accordions, or only strings without the soundbox (guitar and double bass). More recent types are independent of classical musical instruments, for example the *claviphone*.

II Electric musical instruments, whose tone is produced electrically. With these instruments the pitch, volume and timbre of the tone have their counterparts in the frequency, amplitude and harmonic spectrum of the electric wave, which is changed into audible sound by means of an electro-acoustic transducer. They are subdivided into polyphonic instruments and monophonic instruments. According to the tone-generators used, the polyphonic instruments are further classified into electrophonic instruments and electronic instruments.

Electrophonic instruments use electromagnetic ro-

tary generators and the mechanical vibrations are replaced with a rotating phonic wheel. Into this category fall the *Hammond organ*, the new Czechoslovak-made organ and also the organ of the *Pipeless type*. Electronic instruments, on the other hand, have only electronic tone-generators, which means that the tone frequency is produced in the valve without any acoustic vibrations. In this second category are the *Baldwin organ*, the *Connsonata organ*, the *Minshall organ* and the *pianorgan*, as well as the *jonika*.

Monophonic electronic instruments include, in addition to some historic ones such as the tereminvox, trautonium and others, the *melodica, bassophone, electronium, claviolina* and a number of others.

III Electric musical instruments combined with classical instruments. These are the *electronium PI* and the *Hohner-vox*.

It is not possible to describe all the technical details of individual electric musical instruments, and the reader will certainly find more information in specialized publications. But it may be interesting to describe, at least in brief, some well-known types.

The accordion is losing ground in modern jazz, mainly because its tone and accompaniment chords no longer meet the diverse demands of modern jazz modulation. But electricity helps to overcome this trouble. Instead of placing the accordion close to the microphone, a piezoelectric crystal is built in. Weak electric currents generated in the crystal are first amplified and then conveyed into the loudspeaker. Special devices can produce such interesting sound effects that the layman would never believe he is listening to an accordion. In the melodic part of the instrument each tone is picked up individually. Each reed is equipped with a tiny pick-up which is connected with the amplifier, so that the tones are not adversely affected by sound interference from other parts of the mechanism of the accordion.

The *claviphone* is a portable keyboard instrument, its tone being produced by plucking tuned steel reeds equipped with electromagnetic pick-ups. Some amplifiers in the claviphone have tremolos and then, if the musician controls the dynamics properly by means of a pedal, it is possible to imitate some registers of the electrophonic organ.

The group of polyphonic instruments, which use as generators electromagnetic pick-up from phonic wheels includes the *Hammond organ*.

The designers of the first successful electrophonic *Baldwin organ* aimed to construct an instrument that would replace the pipe organ. They used the formant principle to create the tone-timbres in the registers. Specially designed electronic generators, which produce tones with many high-pitched partial tones, imitate perfectly the sound of the pipe organ. The majority of designers and constructors of electric musical instruments initially attempted to replace, with regard to both sound and technique, classical musical instru-

41

ments. This is still true today of some types of electric organs. But the present course of development indicates that the future role of these instruments does not lie in imitating the sound of classical musical instruments, but in the new and exciting possibilities they offer to the imaginative and creative mind.

The *Connsonata organ* made by the American firm C. G. Conn differs from the Baldwin organ in one very important respect — each tone is produced in a separated oscillator. This construction makes the chord effect possible, but on the other hand the tuning of the instrument is very difficult. An electronic musical instrument made by the American firm Minshall has recently gained much popularity, thanks mainly to its simple construction, small size and low weight, and its subsequent low price. It is called the 'organ' for want of a better word, because it does not have much in common with the pipe organ — only the playing technique and the sound character of some registers. An instrument that can be used both for organ and light music has been made in the German Democratic Republic and is called the *jonika*. It has eighteen registers and keyboard with the compass of six octaves. One of the most recent electronic musical instruments is the *pianorgan* designed in Great Britain. Its keyboard has two parts — the right with piano-type keys and compass of three and a half octaves, while the left one has buttons like the accordion and supplies bass accompaniment.

In addition to monophonic electronic musical instruments, most of which are now merely of historical interest, new constructions and systems with a wide range of timbres are being introduced and widely used. Most of them resemble the keyboard accordion without the bass buttons, and their bellows have a twofold function — they contain the sophisticated mechanism and at the same time control the sound volume. This group includes the *bassophone*, which plays the bass accompaniment only, and the *electronium* built by the German firm Hohner. The electronium is also used in a modified form known as the *electronium PI*, as a complementary instrument to the piano or to some other classical keyboard instrument. The sound volume is controlled by means of a knee-lever. The *Hohner-vox* is a combination of the electronium and the accordion and can be played in three ways: as an accordion, as an electronium or as a combination of both.

The present age of technical and scientific revolution is exerting considerable influence upon the creative activity of musicians and composers. They are trying to find new means of expression, though it is logical that a new movement in art cannot be based upon a mere quantity of material, but depends first and foremost on a new and revolutionary concept. Until recently the musical tone, this amazing creation of man's genius, had been known only in the form produced by classical musical instruments. The electric musical instruments are one of the contributory factors in the birth and development of a new kind of musical art whose peak is yet to be reached. But their present existence cannot and must not be denied, writes the German scholar Erich Valentin, and their importance for the further development of music may be as great as that of nuclear physics for other branches of science. Only the future will decide what will be a menace and what will be a boon. These new and revolutionary musical instruments represent the first breakthrough into a world of sounds which is not in the least suggestive of the ancient ideas and inspirations that gave rise to the whole edifice of music and the structure of musical instruments. Very great endeavours will admittedly be needed before they can effectively communicate true art to the listener, but there are no grounds to challenge Arnold Schönberg's prophecy to Jörg Mager: 'This is the revolutionary turning-point in music'.

PLATES

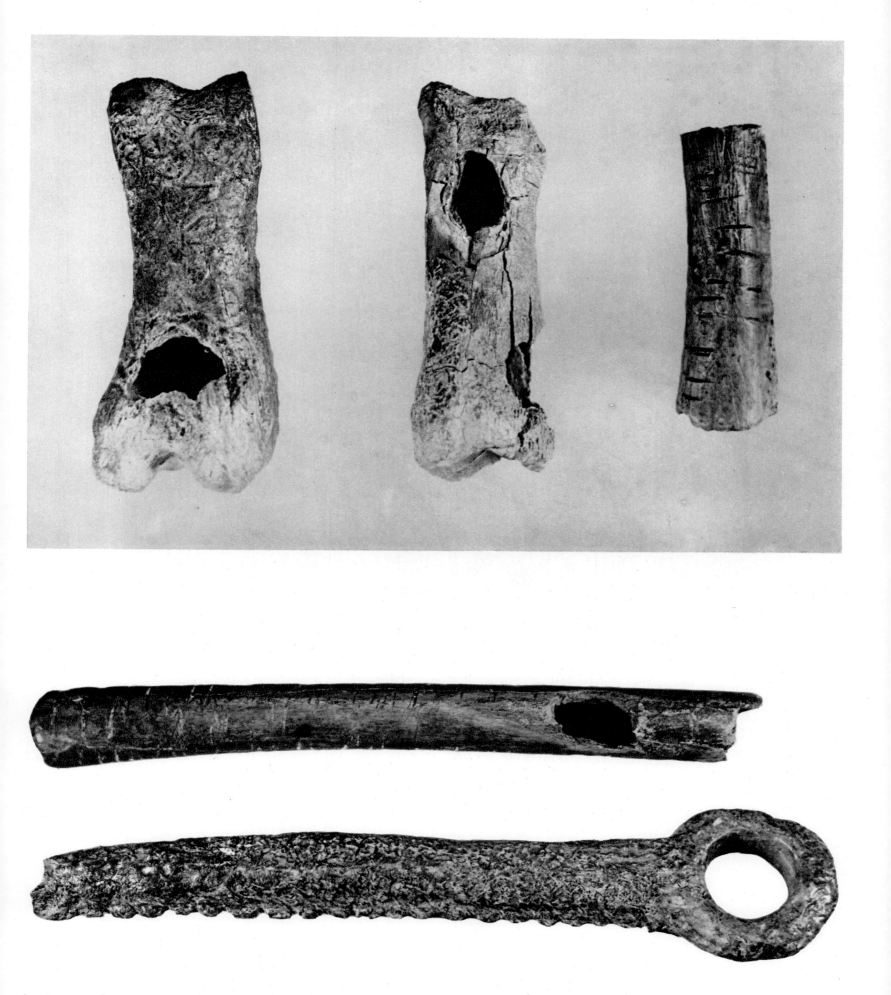

1   Signal whistles dating from the Lower Paleolithic period

2—3   Whistle and scraper dating from the Lower Paleolithic period

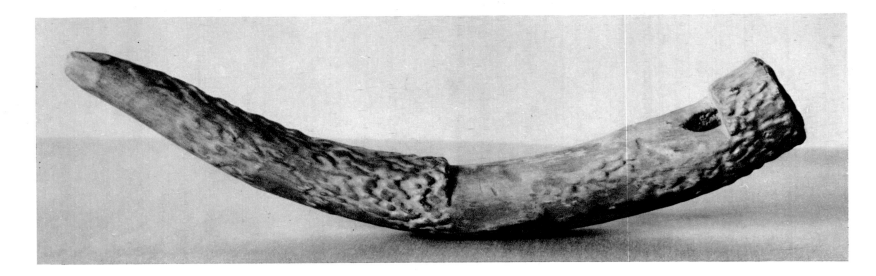

4 Whistle of the first or second century AD
5 Rattles of about the eighth century BC
6—7 Rattles of the eighth century BC
8 Drum with symbolic signs, Upper Paleolithic

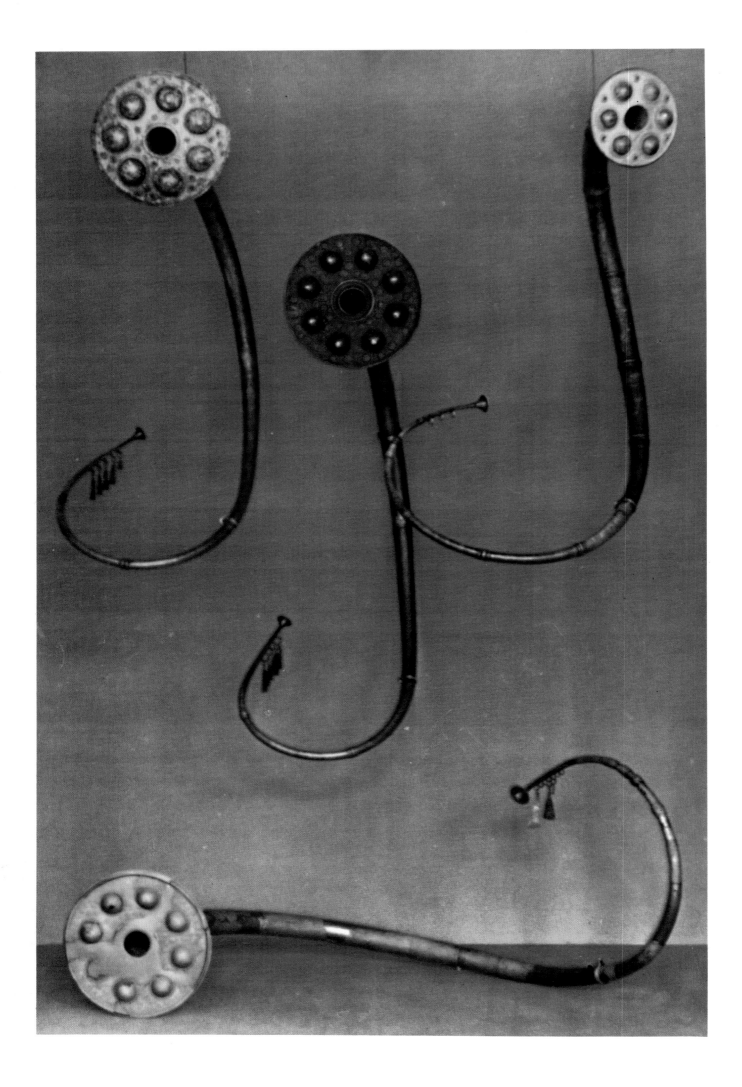

9　Bronze horns, called lurs, from the Late Bronze Age

10　Bronze figurine of a trumpeter, first century BC

11　Whistle from the last quarter of the ninth century AD

12 Hittite guitar on a stone relief dating from about 1350 BC

13 Lyre on a Semitic tomb painting dating from 1920—1900 BC

14 Big Sumerian drum, middle of the third millennium BC

15 Sumerian lyre on
a relief from the royal
palace at Tello, c. 2400
BC

16 Arched harp, lute,
double flute and lyre
on an Egyptian tomb
painting, c. 1420—1411
BC

17 Double aulos and
lyre on a mural
painting in an Etruscan
tomb, first third of the
fifth century BC

18   Aulos on a Greek vase, c. fifth century BC

19   Harp, lyre and double flutes on a relief from the royal palace at Nineveh, c. seventh century BC

20 Egyptian lute and harp of the Eighteenth Dynasty
21 Frame drum, lyres and cymbals on an Assyrian relief, c. 668—627 BC
22 Egyptian harp of the Eighteenth Dynasty

23 Egyptian angular harp of the Nineteenth
Dynasty

24 Egyptian lyre of the Eighteenth Dynasty

25 Bell of a silver trumpet with a wooden
guard from the tomb of Tutankhamen, 1320 BC

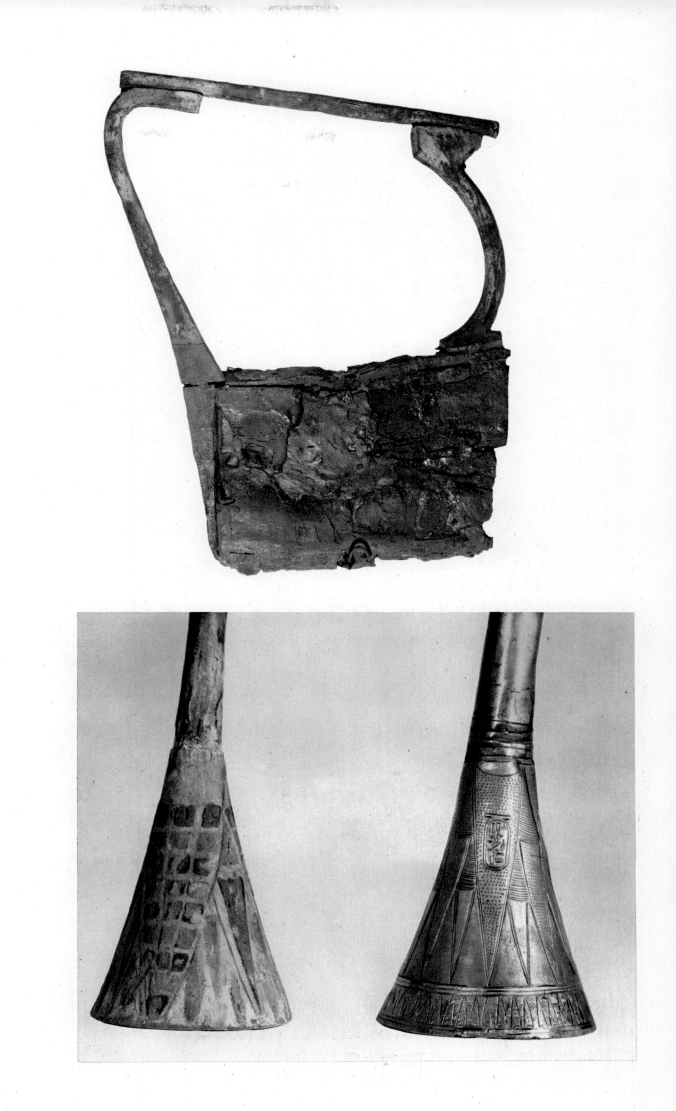

26   Celtic military trumpets, known as karnyx, on a silver vessel of the Later Iron Age

27   Harp, kithara and lyre on a Greek vase, end of the fifth century BC

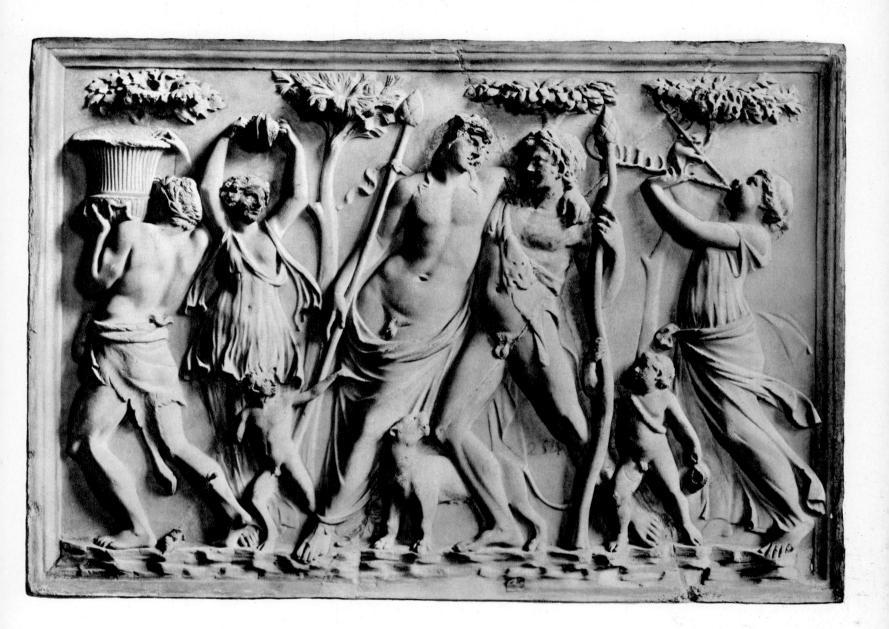

28 Satyr with foot clappers and cymbals, on a Roman sculpture
29 Cymbals and aulos on a Roman marble relief, AD 50

30 Kithara on an ivory plate, fifth century .
31 Roman warriors' trumpets, called buccina, on a stone relief, 109 AD

32　Tibia, small cymbals and tambourine on a Pompeian mosaic, first century BC

33　Lyre on a mural painting from the Augustan age

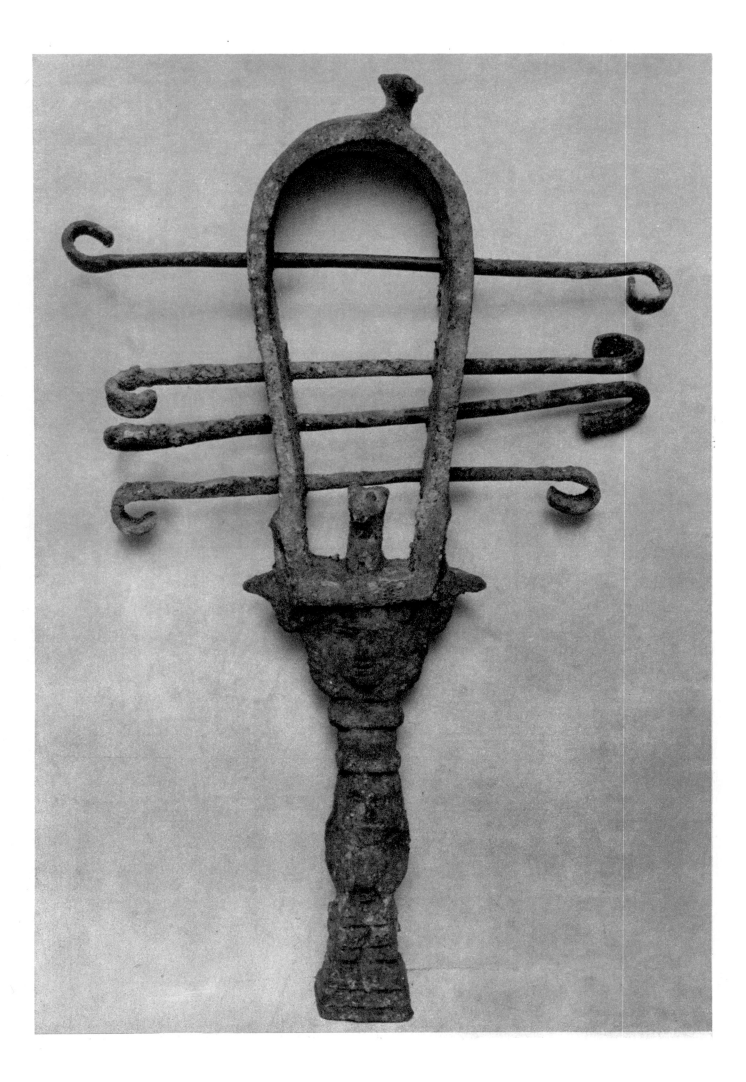

34—6   Musical instruments from Pompeii: rattle (sistrum) and buccina with cymbals

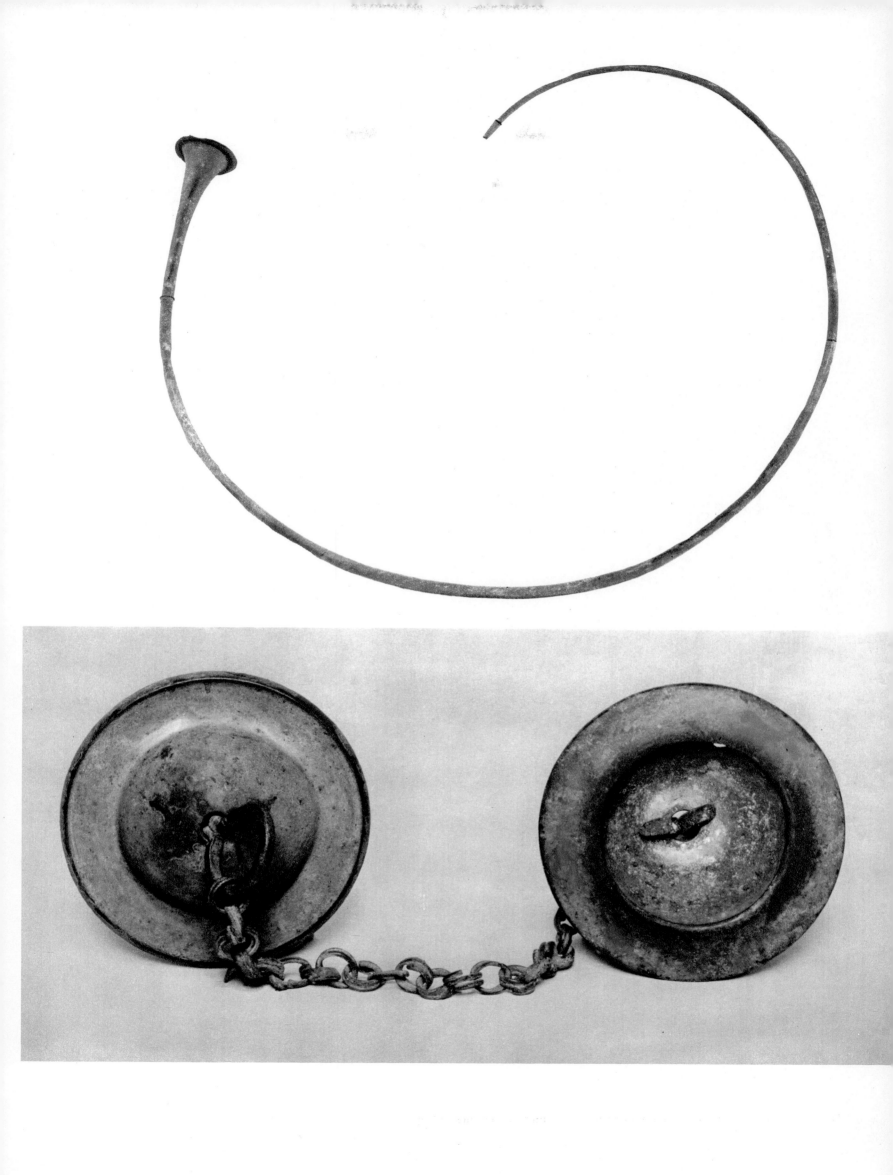

37 Roman organ or hydraulis from Pompeii;
the organ pipes are seen to the right

38 Horn, clappers, harps, lyre and trumpet
(called lituus) in the Bible of Charles the Bald,
ninth century

39—41 Roland's horns, ninth and tenth centuries

42   Above: musical instruments for playing sacred music — monochord, chimes, organ, harp, Panpipes and cornett; below: musical instruments used for secular music — rebec, horn and drum; from the Psalter of Abbot St Remigius, twelfth century

46–7   Harp, Bohemian wing, fiddle and cistra in the Passional
of Abbess Kunhuta, 1319–21

48–51   Horn, fiddle, trumpet and one-hand flute with tabor in
the Latin Bible known as the Jaroměř Bible; end of the thirteenth
century

xul . . .
ton . .
do le . . .
te pst li . . .
tety . . .
psal . . .

dum cum cythara B . . .
menia tuba: in insigni d . . .
nitatis nre Q ula pcep . . .
est: z iudicium deo iacob . . .

52 Drum and trumpet in a miniature from the 'Liber viaticus' of Jan of Středa;
second half of the fourteenth century

53 Drum, flute, shawm, psaltery, two fiddles and bagpipes
in the Codex of the Manesse family, early fourteenth century

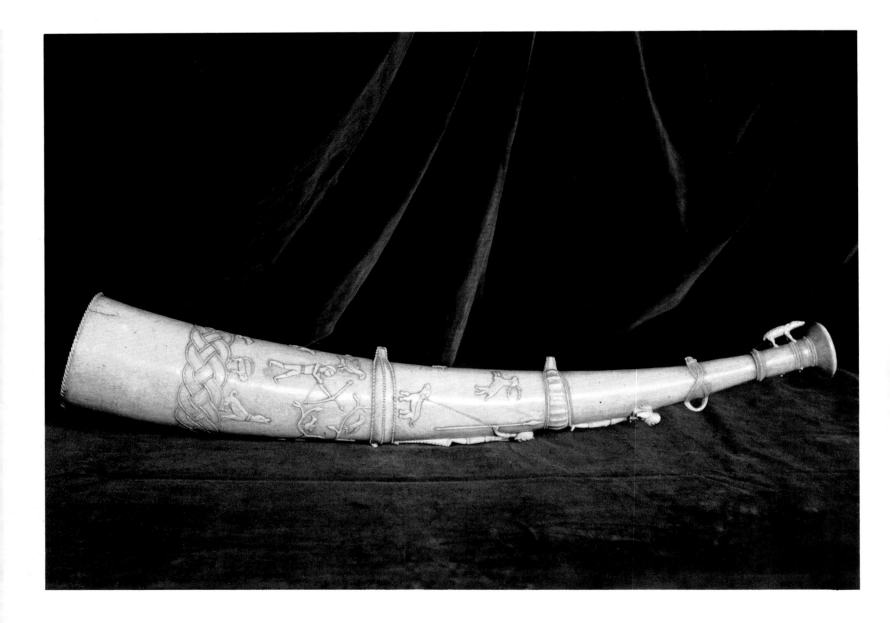

54—6 Fourteenth-century oliphant and details of its decoration

57 Psaltery harp, chimes and psaltery from Velislav's Bible, 1340
58 Bohemian wing, cistra, fiddle and psaltery from Velislav's Bible, 1340

59 Decachordum (ten-stringed), crot, horn and trumpets from Velislav's Bible, 1340

60 Psaltery harp from a breviary of 1342

61 Organ in the Bologna breviary, middle of the fourteenth century

62 Psaltery harp, one-hand flute with tabor and psaltery from the Bible of King Wenceslas IV, late fourteenth century

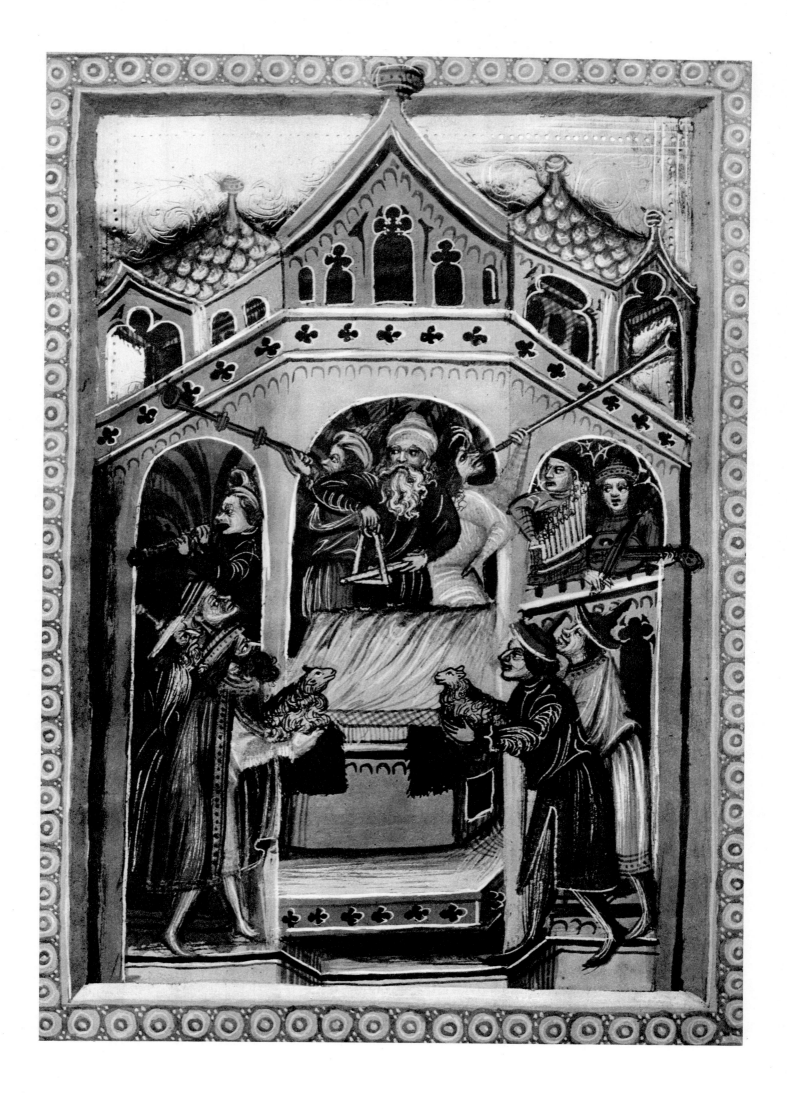

63 Shawm, trumpets, triangle, organ and fiddle from the Bible of King Wenceslas IV, late fourteenth century

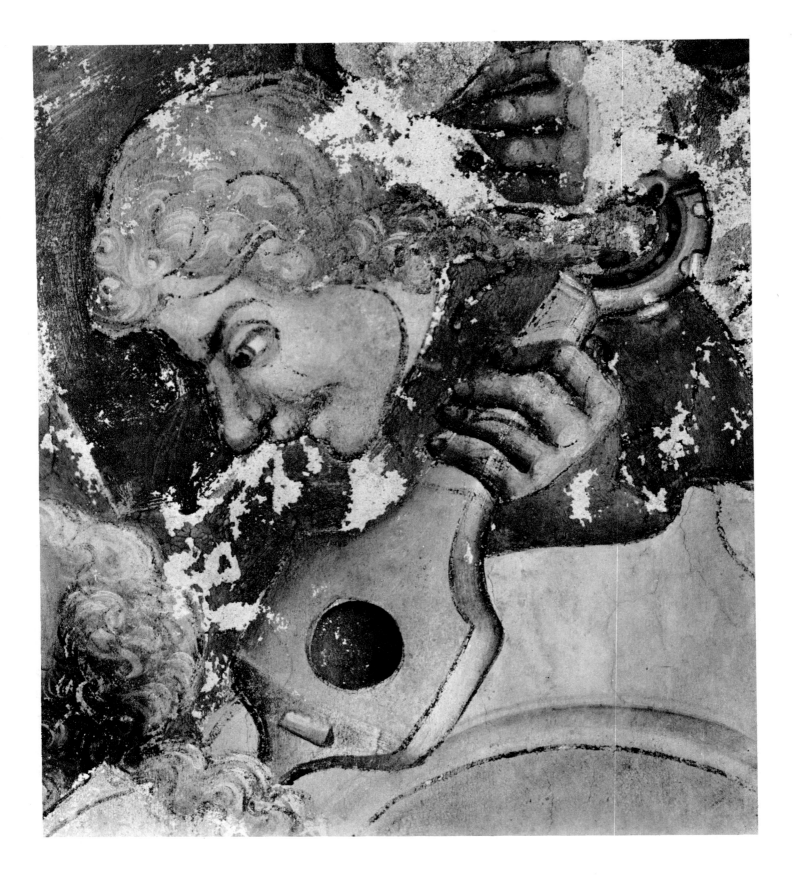

64 Latin guitar (guitara latina): detail of a mural painting at Karlštejn Castle, c. 1360—70

65 Fiddle: detail of a mural painting at Karlštejn Castle, c. 1360—70

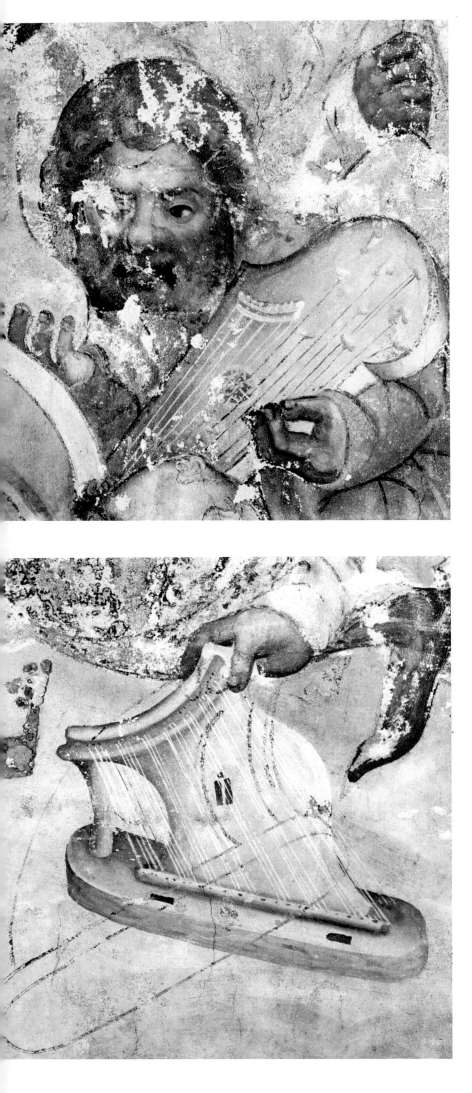

66–9 Bohemian wing, psaltery, psaltery harp and guitara morisca: details of a mural painting at Karlštejn Castle, c. 1360–70

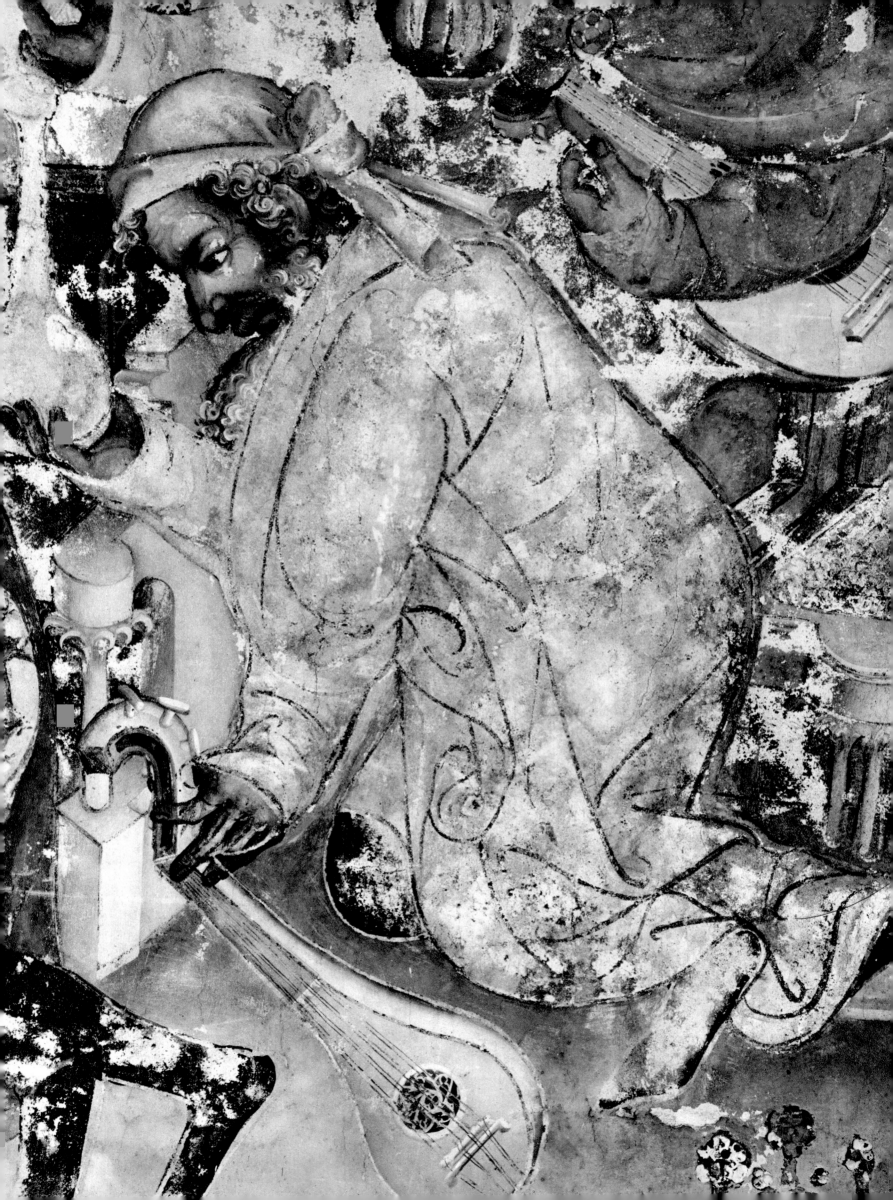

70 Hand-bells, mandora, fiddle and Bohemian
wing in Tomáš Štítný: Six Little Books on Christian
Matters, c. 1376

71—2 Lute, shawm and trumpet from the Krumlov
Volume, early fifteenth century

73—4 Horn and bladder-pipe: detail of a mural
painting at Karlštejn Castle, c. 1360—70

75 Women with mandoras: Italian marble relief, 1431–8

76 Dancing children with cymbals: Italian marble relief, 1431–8

77 Dulcimer, positive, horn, lute, harp, fiddle, one-hand flute with tabor, triangle,
cross flute and bagpipes on a French sixteenth-century tapestry

78 Fiddle, psaltery, lute, tambourine, portative, clappers, bagpipes, shawm,
drums and trumpets in a fourteenth-century book illustration

79 Harp, hurdy-gurdy, psaltery and fiddle from a Calendarium of Irish origin. End of the thirteenth or beginning
of the fourteenth century

80 Drums, bladder-pipe and organ in the Lobkovice Breviary, 1494

81 Pommers and trumpets (one trumpet is S-shaped) in the Richenthal Chronicle, 1464

82 Clavicytherium: detail of a wooden altar, late fifteenth century

83 Bells, triangle, recorder, jingles, trumpet, harp, shawm, fiddle, lute, organ, dulcimer, mandora, white (straight) cornett, harp, tromba marina, psaltery, drums, chimes, clavichord, bell and hurdy-gurdy, from a codex of 1448

84 Drums, fiddle, horn, triangle, lute and bagpipes in a miniature from the Olomouc Bible, 1417

85 Violas da gamba and da braccio on the Isenheim Altar by M. Grünewald, late fifteenth century

86—7 Psaltery and lute, lyre and rebec: marble reliefs by A. di Duccio, c. 1450

88—9 Harp, lute and trumpets from the Litoměřice Hymn Book, 1520

90—1   Harp and viola da braccio, black (curved) cornett and bass pommer
from the Mladá Boleslav Gradual, 1570—2

92   Fiddle, mural painting by Pinturicchio, c. 1454—1513

MVSICA

93　Lute, harp, hurdy-gurdy, triangle, pommer, drum, trumpet: detail from a painting by H. Bosch
(c. 1450—1516)

94 Viola da braccio, flute, lute, black cornett, harp, viola da gamba:
detail of a painting by an unknown Italian master of the sixteenth century

95 From the left: clavichord, trombones, cornett, cross flute, shawm, viol, trombone, cornett, cross flute,
lute (the woman next to the clavichord player is playing a viola da gamba), by H. Müelich, 1548

96 Tenor, bass and double bass windcap shawms, late sixteenth century

97 Slide trumpet (tromba da tirarsi), cornetts, recorders and crumhorns, from a painting by an unknown Czech artist, 1520

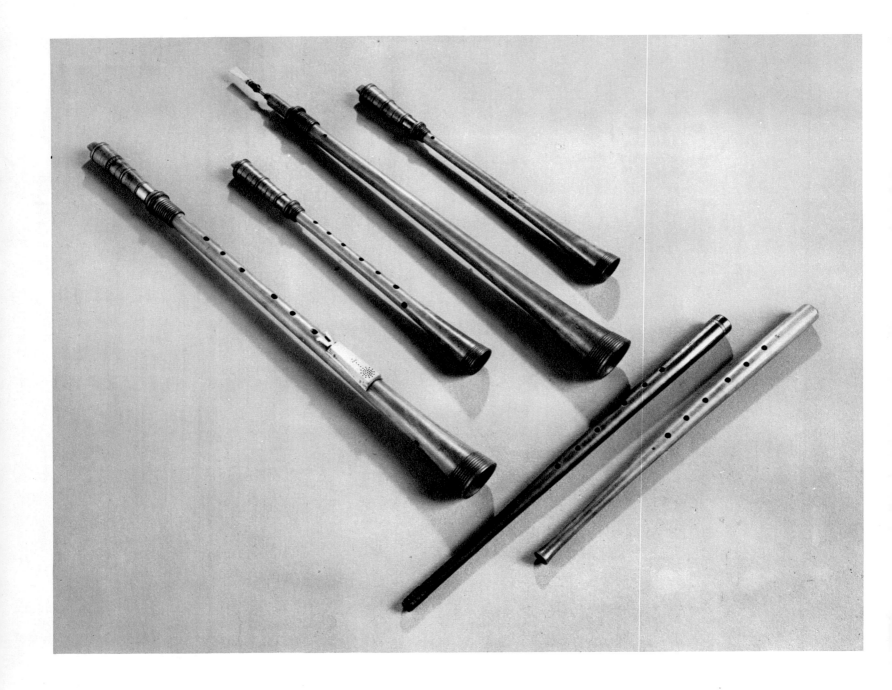

98 Windcap shawms and cornetts, late sixteenth century

99—100 Pommer, windcap shawm, crumhorn and detail of the windcap, late sixteenth century

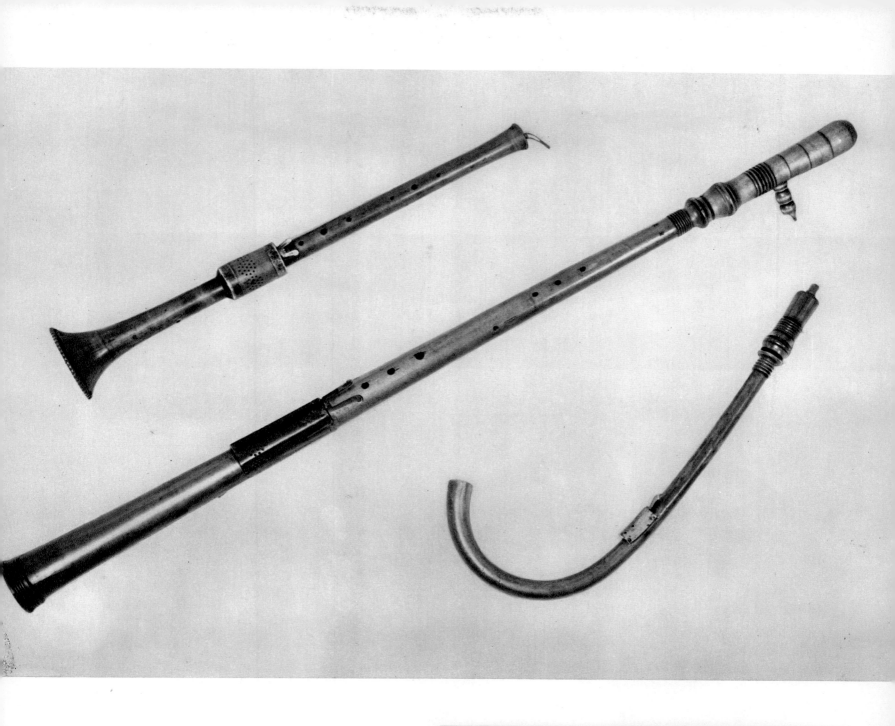

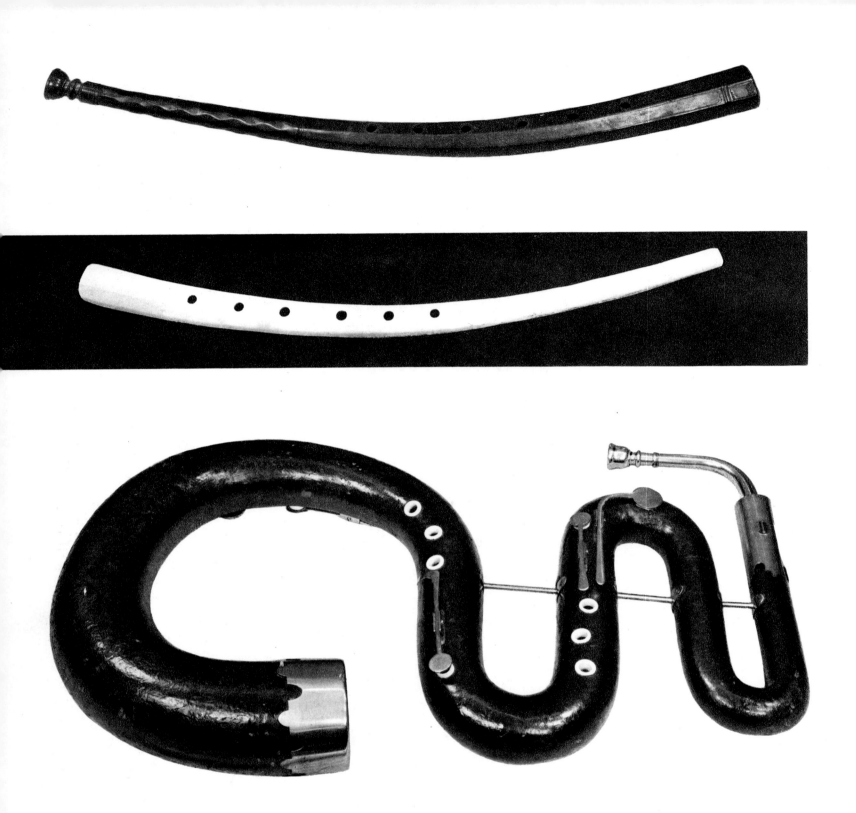

101—3 Black cornett, white cornett, late sixteenth century,
and serpent made by Gerock and Wolf, London, c. 1831

104 Organ, bass viol, black cornett, recorder, tenor viol and tambourine,
Sisto Rosa, called Badalocchio (1581—1647)

105 Regal, descant and alto viols: woodcut dating from 1633

106 Cornett, dulcian and trumpet: woodcut dating from 1633

107 Alto recorder, painting by J. Kupecký (1667-1740)

108 Alto and bass recorders made by P. I. Bresgan in the seventeenth century

109 Flute and lute with a lute case in the background,
by an anonymous master of the sixteenth century

110—11 Alto recorders, seventeenth and eighteenth centuries

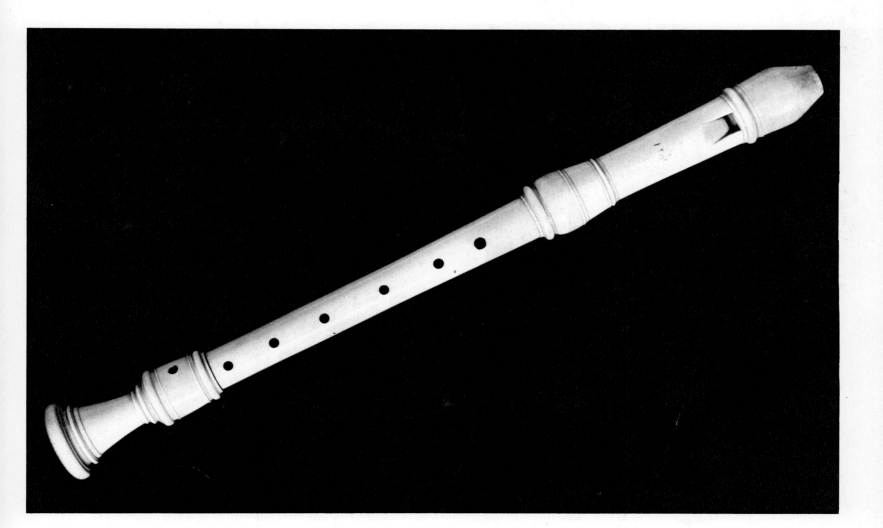

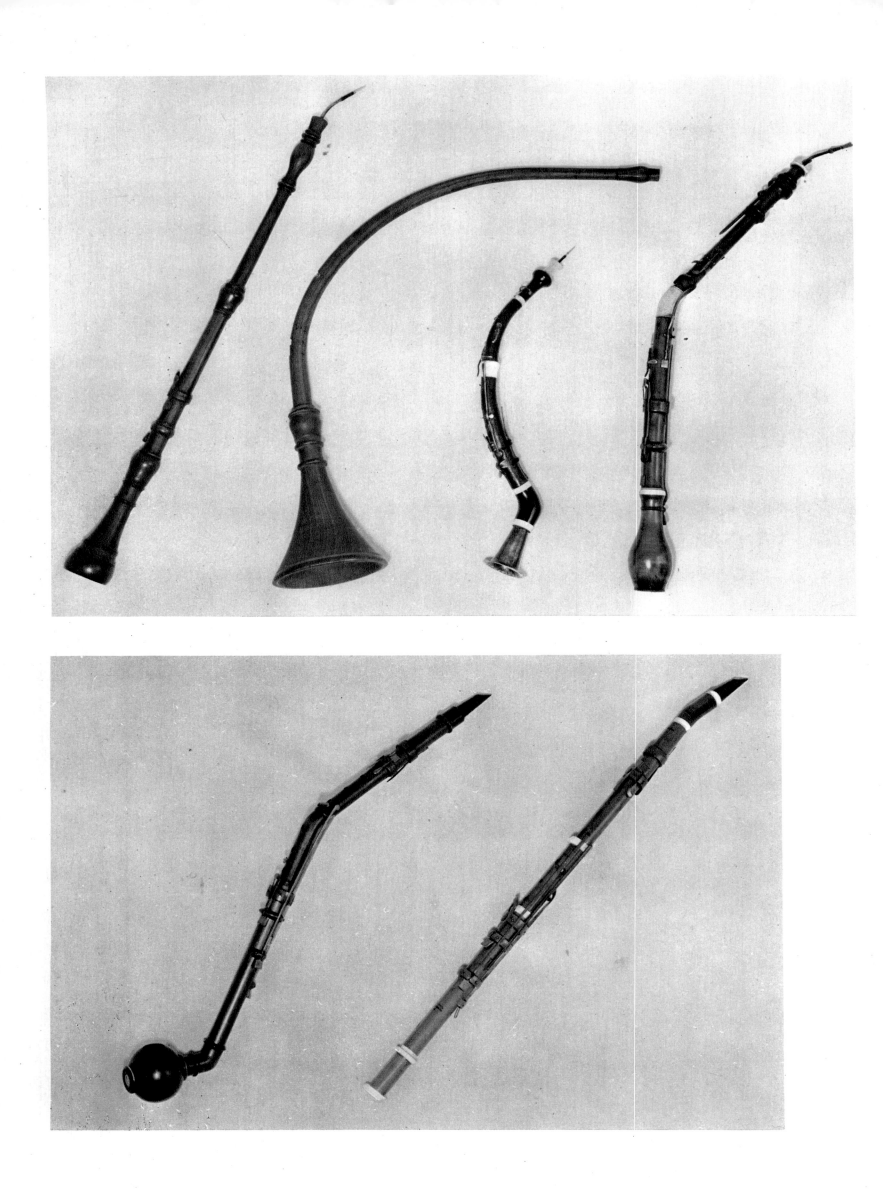

112 Hunting oboe made by Friedrich, seventeenth century, and cors anglais made in Bohemia, seventeenth to nineteenth century

113 Czech basset-horns, nineteenth century

114—15 Czech basset-horns and detail, eighteenth century

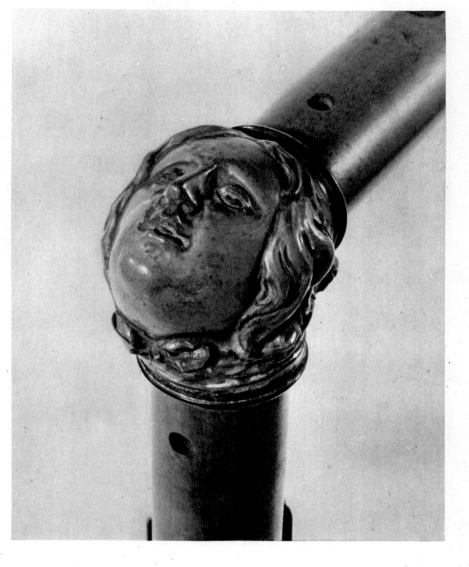

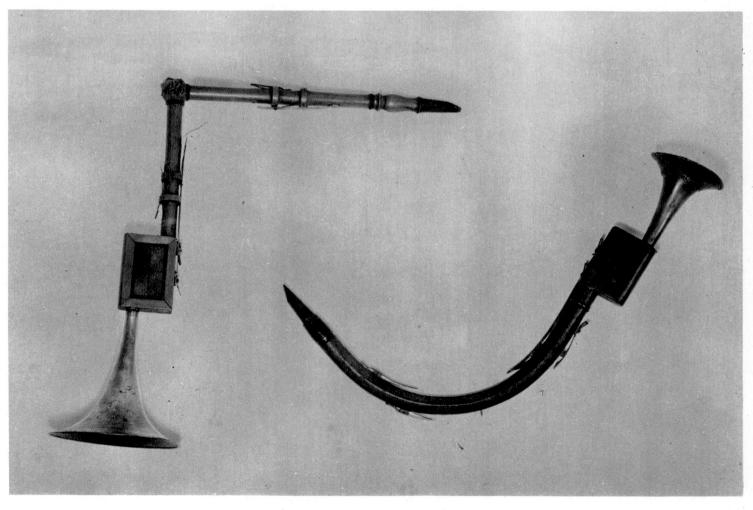

116 Flutes (and daggers), late eighteenth century

117 Eighteenth-century mirlitons

118 Oboe and theorbo lute: detail of a painting by F. X. Verbeeck (1686—1755)

119 Cross flute, violin and recorder by J. Leyster (c. 1610—60)
120 Viola da gamba, trumpet, violin, lute, recorder; J. A. Adolph (1729—80)

121   Trumpets, kettle-drums, black cornetts, violin, lute, bass gamba and organ; J. J. Heinsch (1647—1712)

122   Cross flute made of porcelain, second half of the eighteenth century

123 Silver trumpet and kettle-drum from the English Royal Collections, eighteenth century

124 Trumpet in a painting by J. Verkolje (1650—93)

125   Trumpet made by A. Schnitzer of Nuremberg, 1598

126   Trumpet made by J. W. Haas of Nuremberg, first half of the eighteenth century

127—8   Trumpet made by Bauer of Prague and detail of its decorated ball, eighteenth century

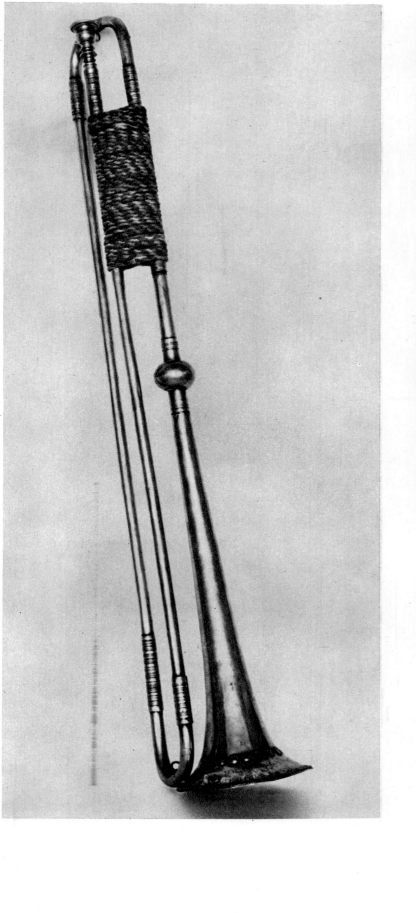

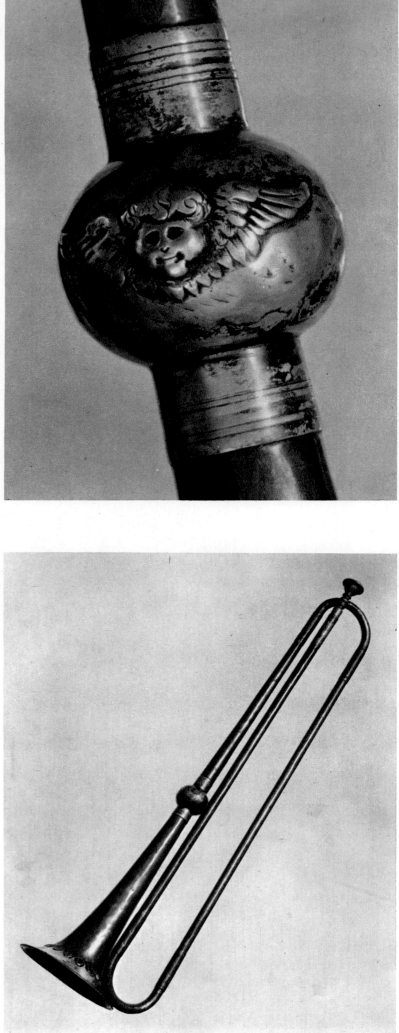

129 Clavichord and tenor viola da gamba by J. Vermeer van Delft (1632—75)

130 Seventeenth-century harpsichord in a painting by Gonzales Coques (1614—84)

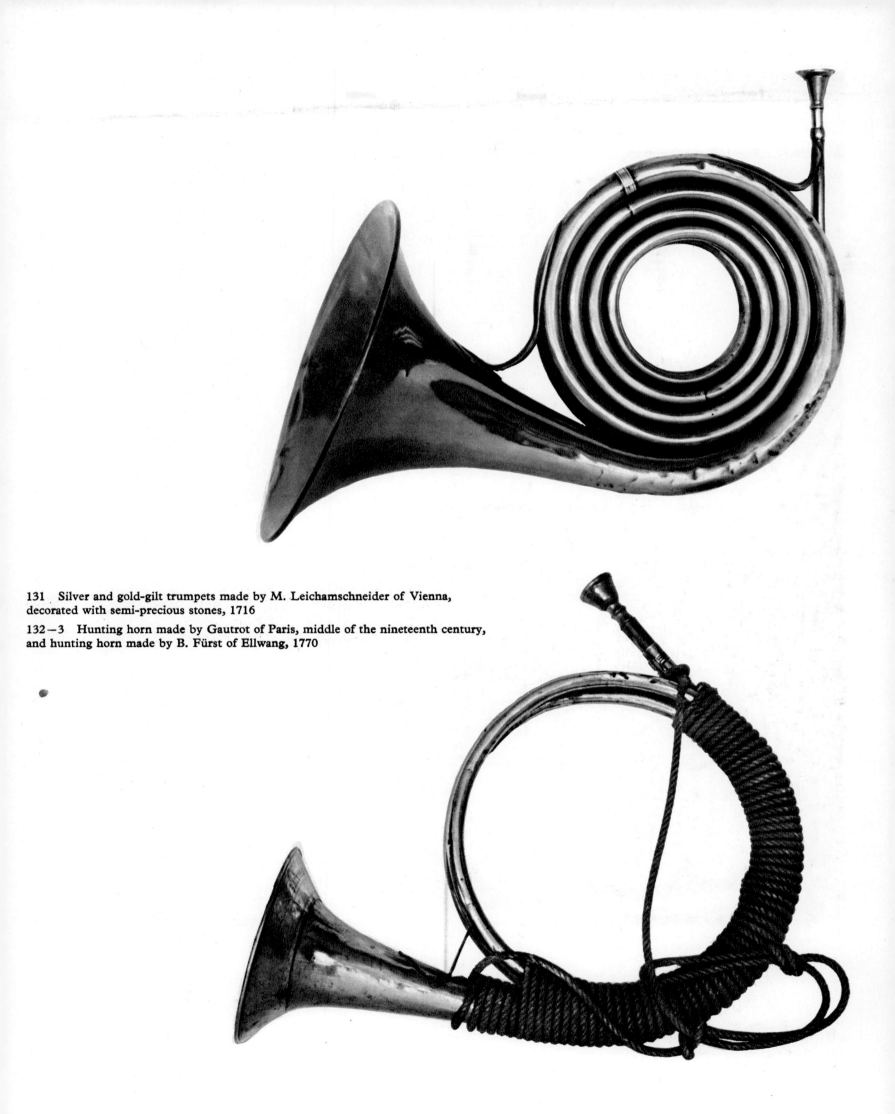

131 Silver and gold-gilt trumpets made by M. Leichamschneider of Vienna, decorated with semi-precious stones, 1716

132—3 Hunting horn made by Gautrot of Paris, middle of the nineteenth century, and hunting horn made by B. Fürst of Ellwang, 1770

134 Organ, flute, violin and violoncello: painting on a goblet, middle of the eighteenth century

135 Harp and French horns: painting on a goblet, middle of the eighteenth century

136 French horn, zither and timpani: engraving on a goblet, c. 1700
137 Bassoon and French horn, Viennese porcelain, eighteenth century

138　Lira da gamba; P. F. Mola (1612—68)

139　Tenor viola da gamba, organ, cross flute, psaltery, lira da braccio by Tintoretto (1518—94)

140 Viola da gamba and lute in a painting by F. Francia (1500)
141 Bass viola da gamba in a painting by E. Lesueur (1617—55)

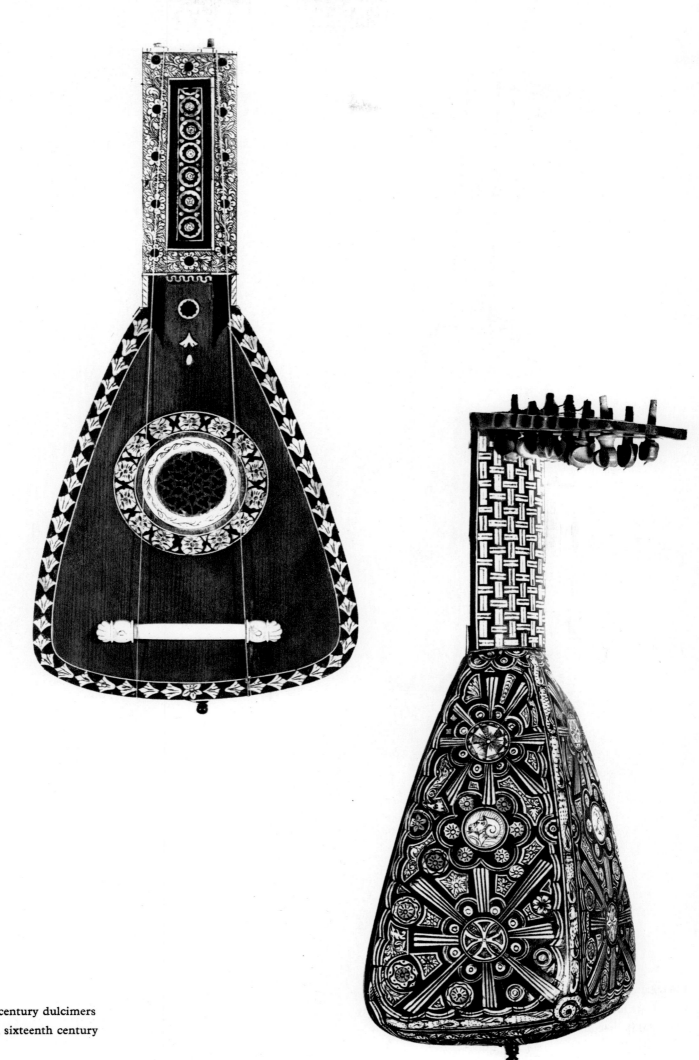

142—3 Seventeenth-century dulcimers
144—5 Soprano lute, sixteenth century

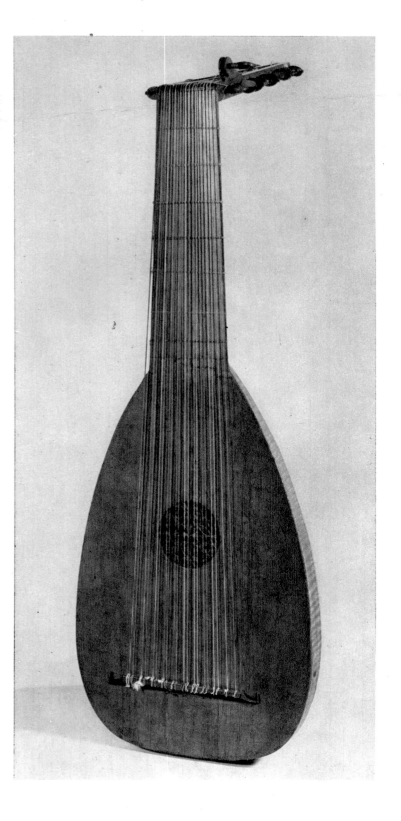

146 Lute made by G. Gerle of Innsbruck, c. 1580

147 Lute made by H. Frey, Bologna, late sixteenth century

148 Fiddle, recorder, lute; E. de Roberti (c. 1450—96)

149—50   Lute and violin, with a detail from a painting by M. da Caravaggio (c. 1560—1609)

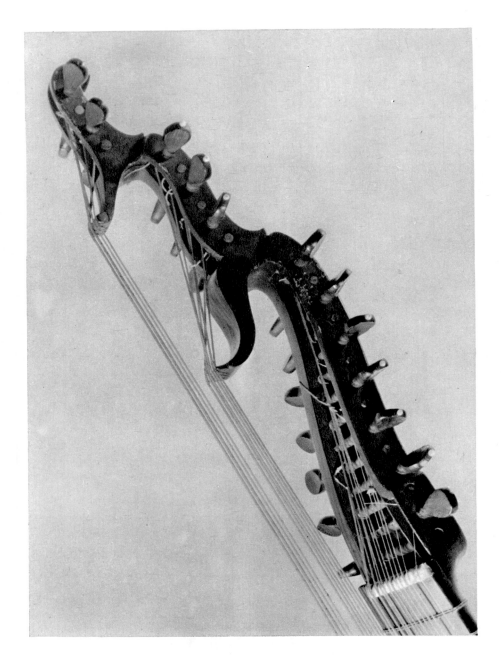

151—2 Theorbo made by M. Brunner of Olomouc
and detail of the pegbox, 1764

153 Theorbo lute by F. Bol (1616—80)

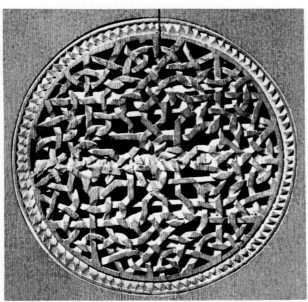

154 Lute, M. Dahl (c. 1700)

155—6 Lute made by
M. Unverdorben of Venice and detail
of the rose, sixteenth century

157—8 Lute made by T. Edlinger
of Prague and detail of the rose,
late seventeenth century

162   Chitarrone made by J. Mantoya de Cardone in 1591

163—4   Chitarrone modelled on the original by M. Schott (1680) and detail of the roses

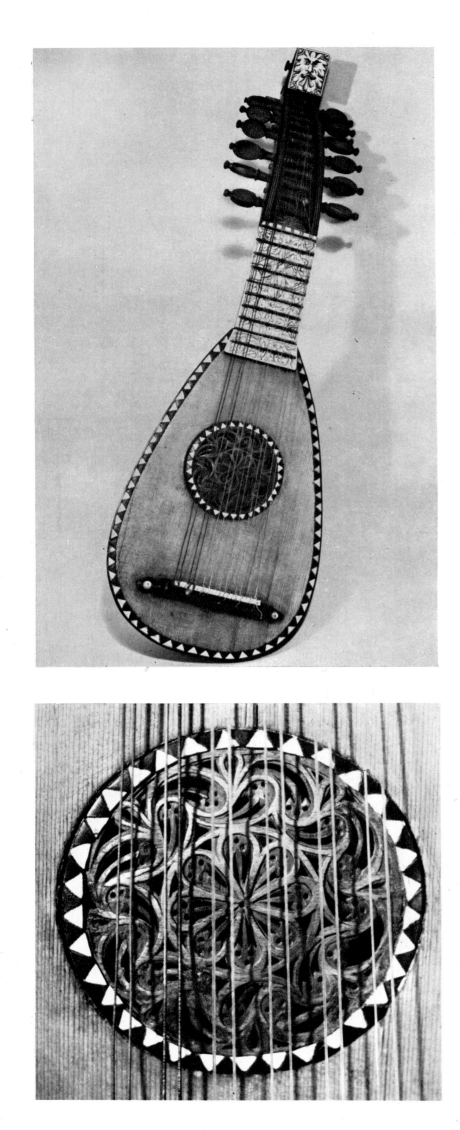

165–6 Pandurine and detail of the rose, 1673

167–8 Mandora made by M. A. Bergonzi of Cremona and detail of the scroll, 1765

169 Neapolitan mandoline made by J. J. Franck of Dresden, 1789

170 Milanese mandoline made by F. Plesber of Milan, 1773

171 Eighteenth-century Italian mandoline

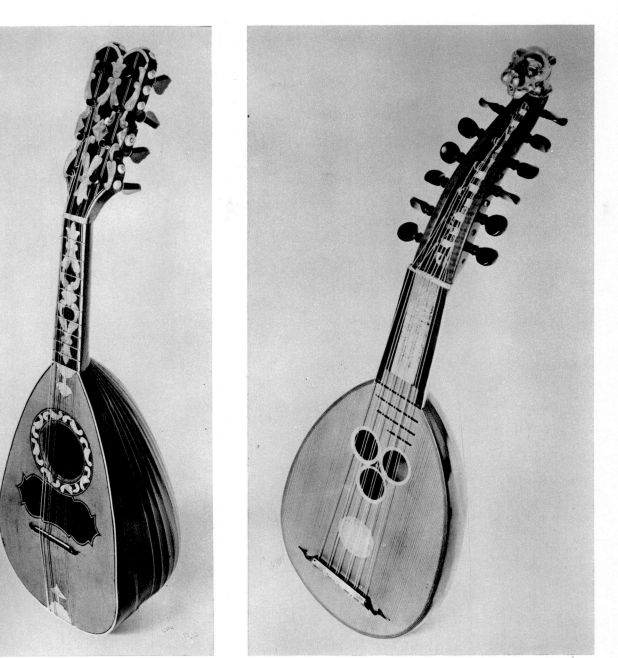

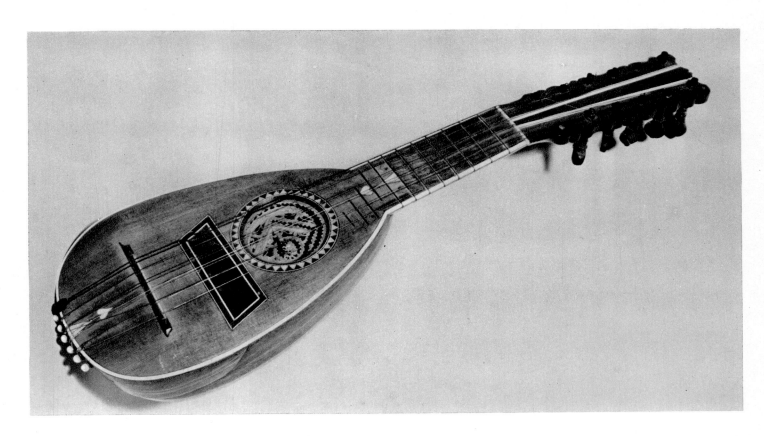

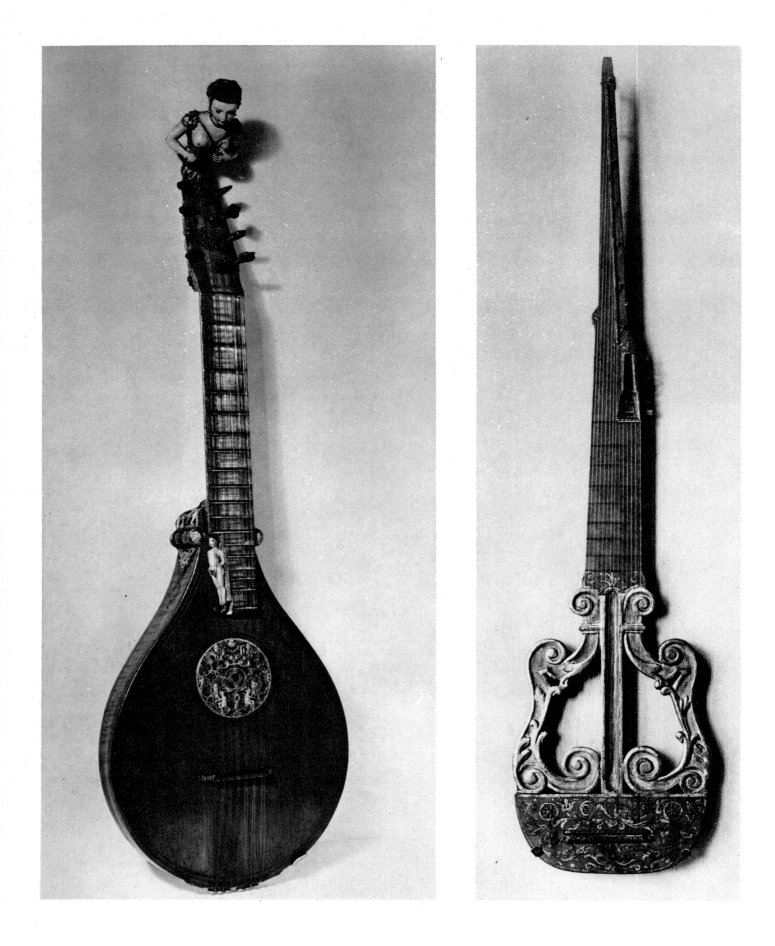

172　Cittern made by G. de Virchi of Brescia
for Archduke Ferdinand of Tyrol, 1574

173　Lyre cittern, sixteenth or seventeenth century

174—5　Bell-cittern probably made by the Hamburg violin-maker
J. Tielke at the turn of the eighteenth century

176 Cittern by G. F. Cipper, eighteenth century

177 Cistra made by M. Zacher, Breslau, 1751

178 Guitar-cittern made by J. M. Willer, Prague, 1799

179 Guitar made by G. Sellas, Venice, first half of the seventeenth century

180 Guitar made by T. O. Hulinzký, Prague, 1754

181 Back of a guitar made by G. Sellas

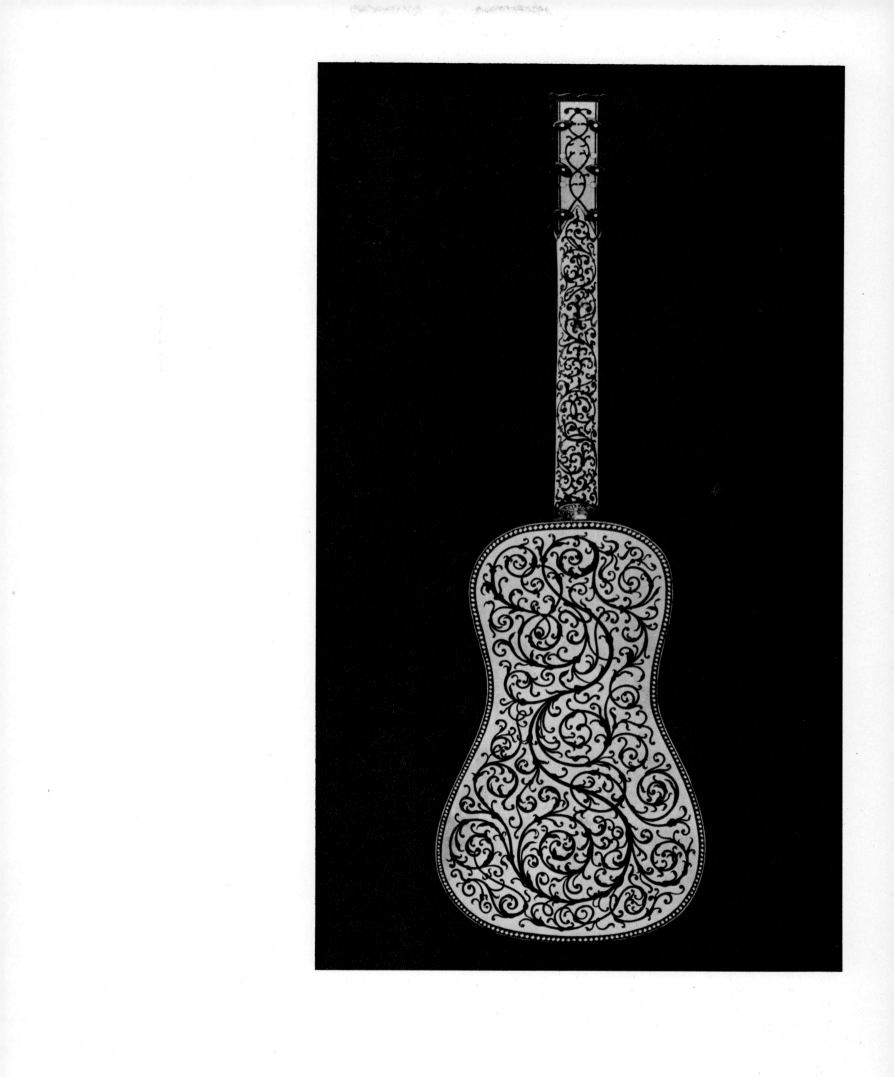

182 Plectrum guitar made by V. Vinaccio, Naples, 1772

183 Detail of a guitar made by J. Tielke (plates 184—5)

184—5 Guitar made by J. Tielke of Hamburg, late seventeenth century

186   Guitar, cross flute, lute by J. Massys, sixteenth century

187—8   Italian chitarra battente, seventeenth century

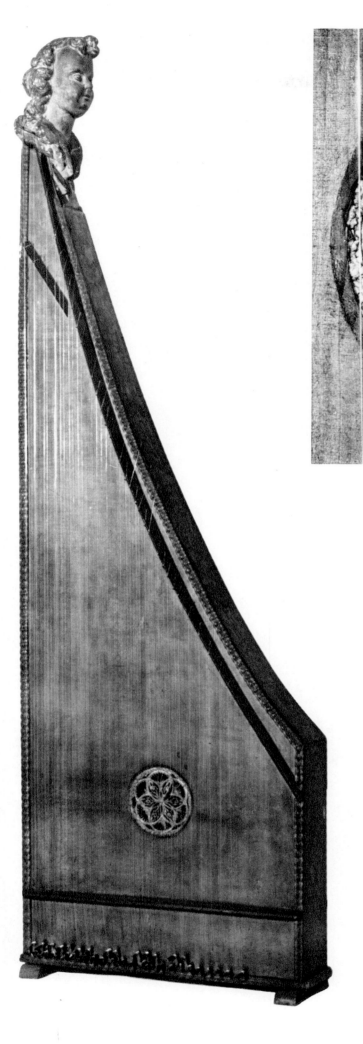

189—90   Guitar made by M. Fux in Vienna
and detail of the rose, 1692

191—2   Seventeenth-century arpanetta and detail of the rose

193–4 Guitar made by J. Pereira-Coelho, 1800
195 Guitar modified by Ritter, nineteenth century
196 Nineteenth-century dital harp

197—9 Pedal harp built by H. Nadermann in Paris 1785 and details
200 Pedal harp with hook action: colour engraving, late eighteenth century

201—2 Modern pedal harp made by A. Červenka in Prague and head of another harp by the same maker

203 Marie Antoinette's 'golden harp', made by Cousineau in Paris, late eighteenth century

204—6 Virginal belonging to Catherine of Brandenburg and details, 1620—30

207 Ottavina spinet, seventeenth century

208 Harpsichord made by Vitus de Trasuntinus, Venice, 1560

209—10 Virginal and a detail of the instrument, 1575

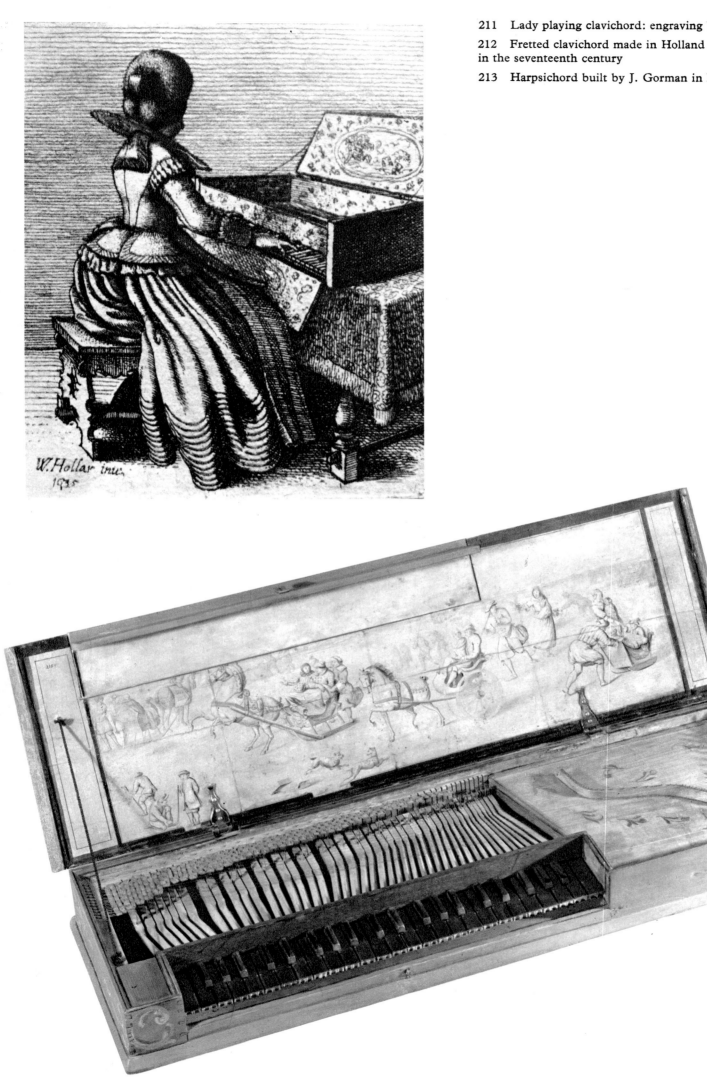

211 Lady playing clavichord: engraving by V. Hollar, 1635

212 Fretted clavichord made in Holland in the seventeenth century

213 Harpsichord built by J. Gorman in Paris, 1738

214 Square piano built by L. Sauer in Prague, early nineteenth century

215 Two-manual harpsichord built by Pietro Todino, Milan, 1675

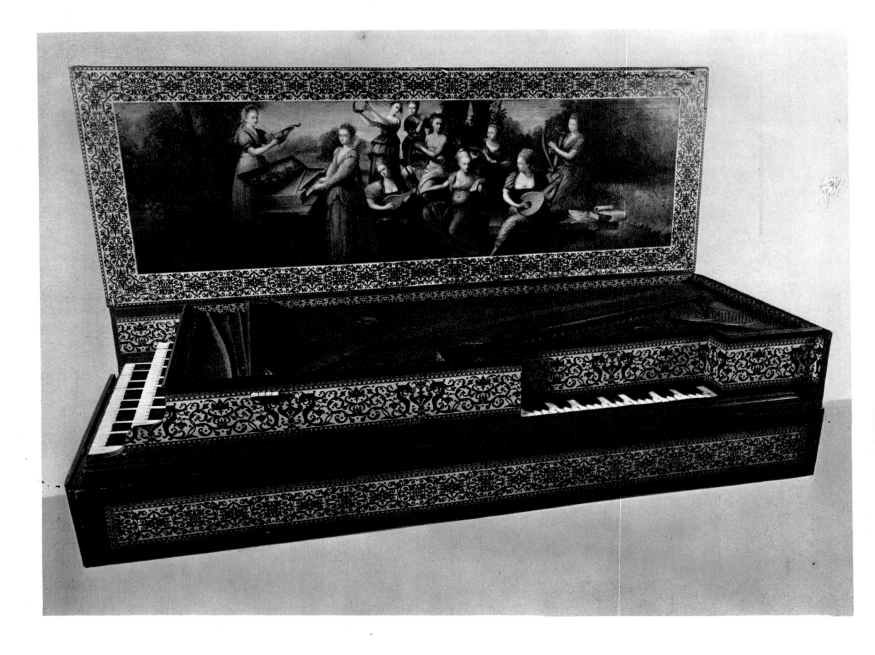

216 Harpsichord-spinet made by J. Ruckers, Antwerp, 1619

217 Seventeenth-century harpsichord

218 Virginal made by J. Ruckers, Antwerp, 1581
219 Lutes, shawms and flutes: detail of a painting on the double virginal made by J. Ruckers in 1581

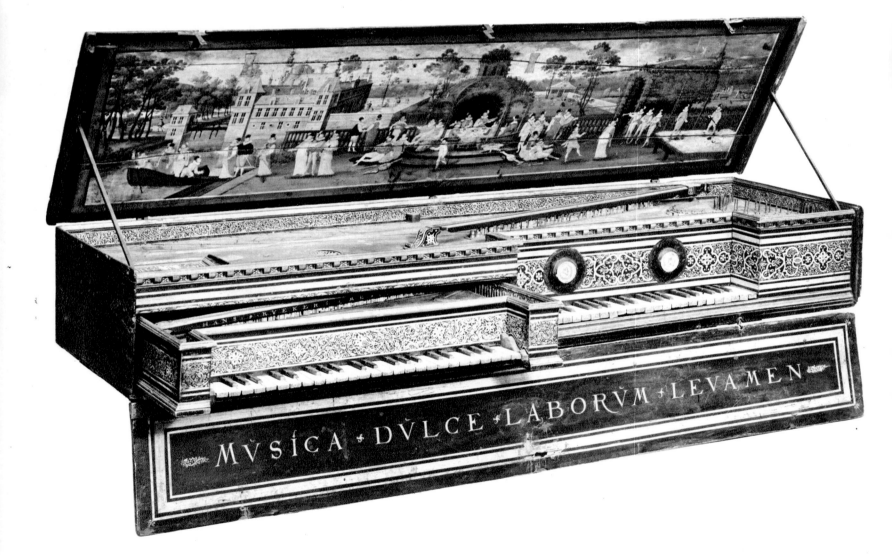

220   Seventeenth-century harpsichord

221 Eighteenth-century hammer piano

222 Harpsichord made by Burkat Shudi
and Johannes Broadwood in London, 1775, which belonged to J. Haydn

223 Eighteenth-century hammer piano

222 Harpsichord made by Burkat Shudi
and Johannes Broadwood in London, 1775, which belonged to J. Haydn

223 Eighteenth-century hammer piano

224 Pyramid piano made by L. Sauer of Prague, early nineteenth century

225 Clavicytherium made by M. Kaiser, mid-seventeenth century

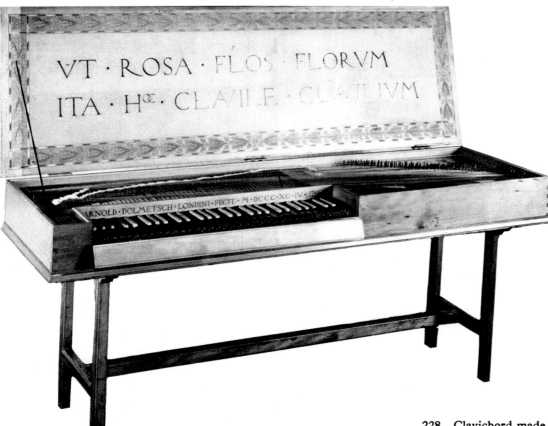

228   Clavichord made by A. Dolmetsch, London, 1894

229   Square piano with pedals made by G. Scappa, Milan, 1804

230   Flute, lute and bumbass; J. Steen (1626—79)

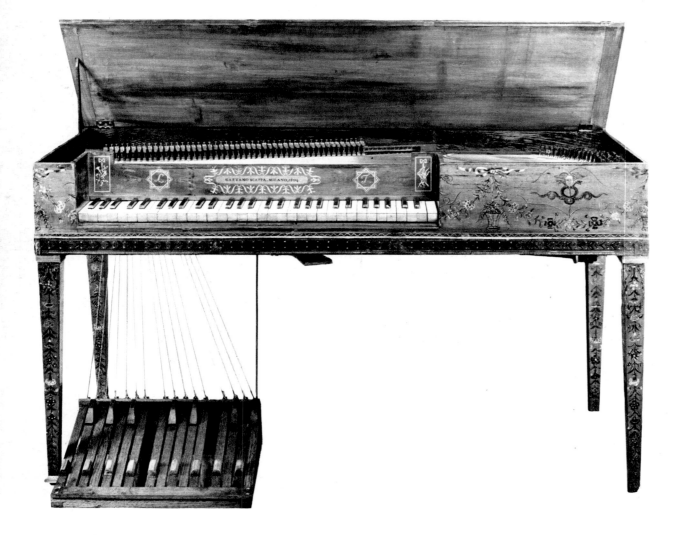

231 Fiddle: detail of a painting of c. 1504

232 Lira da braccio made by J. Andrea, Verona, 1511

233 Lira da braccio: detail of the fresco Parnassus by Raffaello Sanzio (1483—1520) /

234 Viola da braccio by an anonymous master of the sixteenth century
235 Violoncello, lute and violin on a gingerbread mould, late seventeenth century

236—8   Three gambas made by Gasparo da Salò in Brescia,
second half of the sixteenth century

239—40 Viola d' amore made by A. N. Bartl in Vienna,
second half of the eighteenth century

241—2 Viola d'amore and English violetta made
by J. O. Eberle, Prague, 1758 and 1727

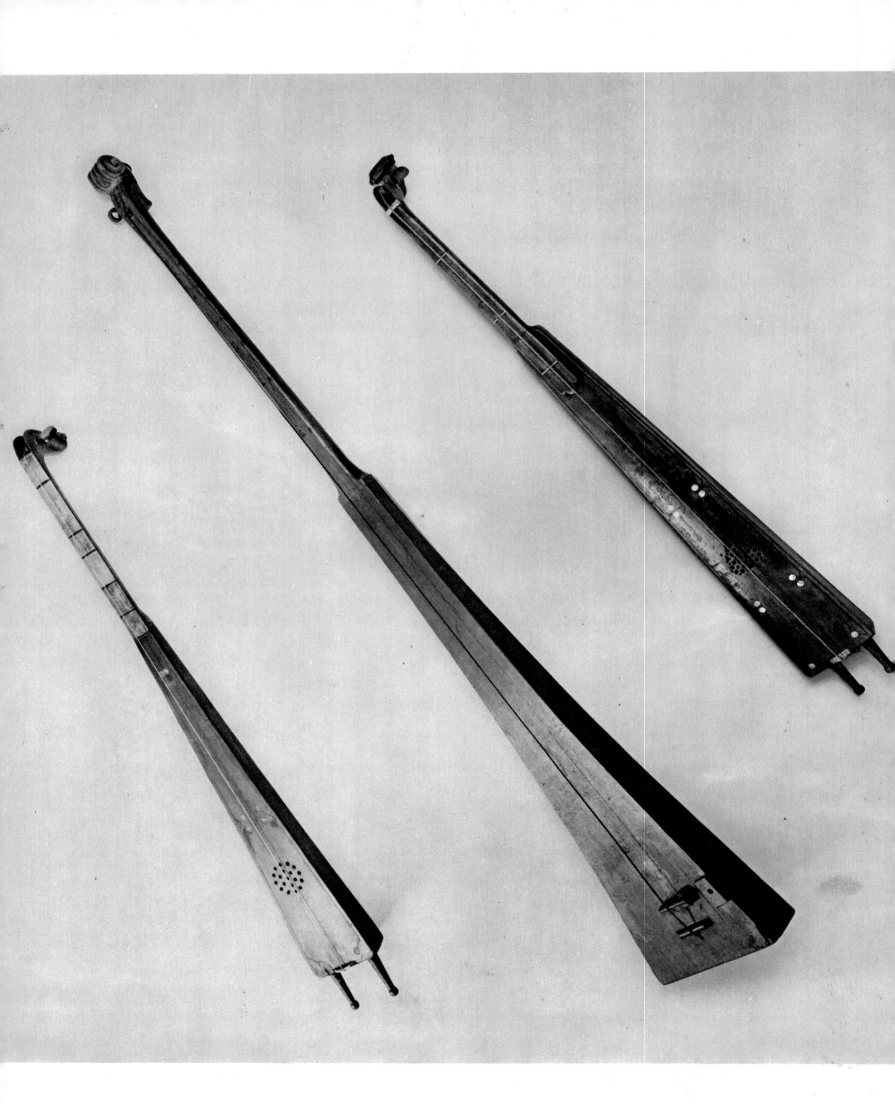

243 Trumscheits (tromba marina), seventeenth and eighteenth century
244—5 Violin made by Giovanni D. Ventura, Venice, 1622

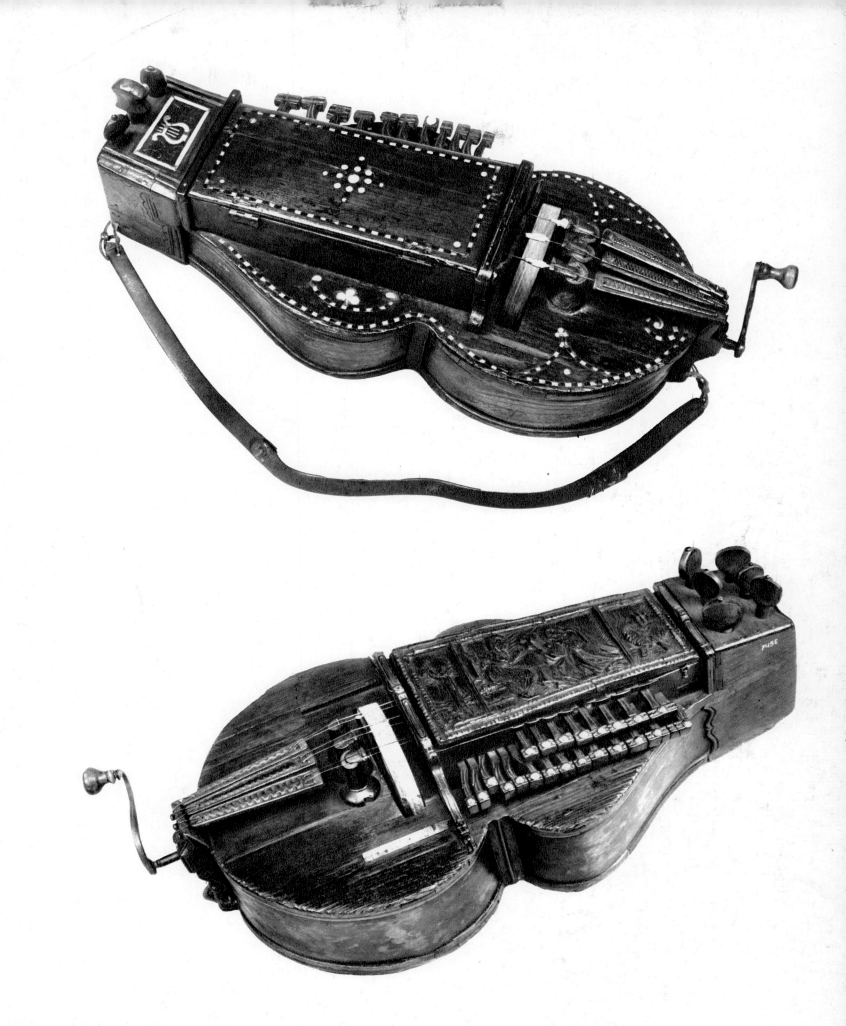

246 Hurdy-gurdy and lute: painting by J. Ochtervelt, eighteenth century

247—8 Czech hurdy-gurdies, eighteenth century

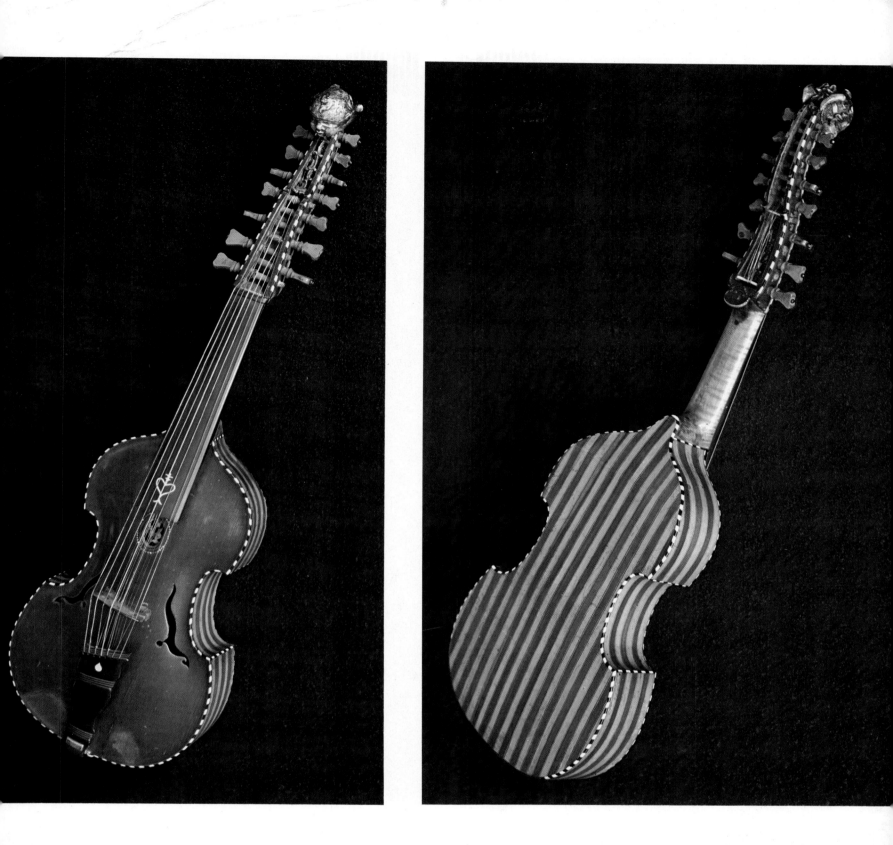

249   Tenor viol: painting by J. Kupecký (1667—1740)
250—1   Viola d'amore made by T. O. Hulinzký, Prague, 1769

252—3　Replica by J. B. Vuillaume of violin by A. Guarneri and detail of its neck

254　Violin, tambourine, trombone, pommer, bass viola da gamba and lute: painting by P. Lastman (c. 1583—c. 1633)

255—6 Kit (small violin played by dancing masters) made by K. B. Dvořák, Prague, nineteenth century

257 Sordine from a lithograph

258—9 Eighteenth-century sordines

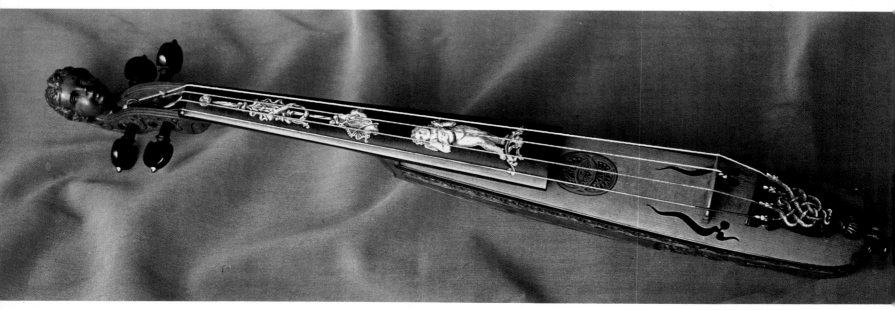

260   Tenor viola da gamba in a painting by J. Verkolje (1650—93)

261—2   Tenor viola da gamba made by J. O. Eberle of Prague
and detail of the neck, 1740

263—4 Tenor quinton made by T. O. Hulinzký of Prague
and detail of the neck and pegbox, 1754

265—6 Viola di bardone (baryton) made by an anonymous
maker in Vienna and detail of the neck and pegbox,
eighteenth century

267—9   Bass viola da gamba (later reconstructed
into a four-stringed instrument) made by J. Tielke, Hamburg, 1687

270   Guitar, flute with tabor, tambourine and triangle,
painting by an anonymous Czech master of the seventeenth century

271   Side drum of the Prague brewers' guild, 1639
272   Glass harmonica made by C. F. Pohl at Chřibská in Bohemia, early nineteenth century
273   Bells called the 'Chinese Pavilion', eighteenth century

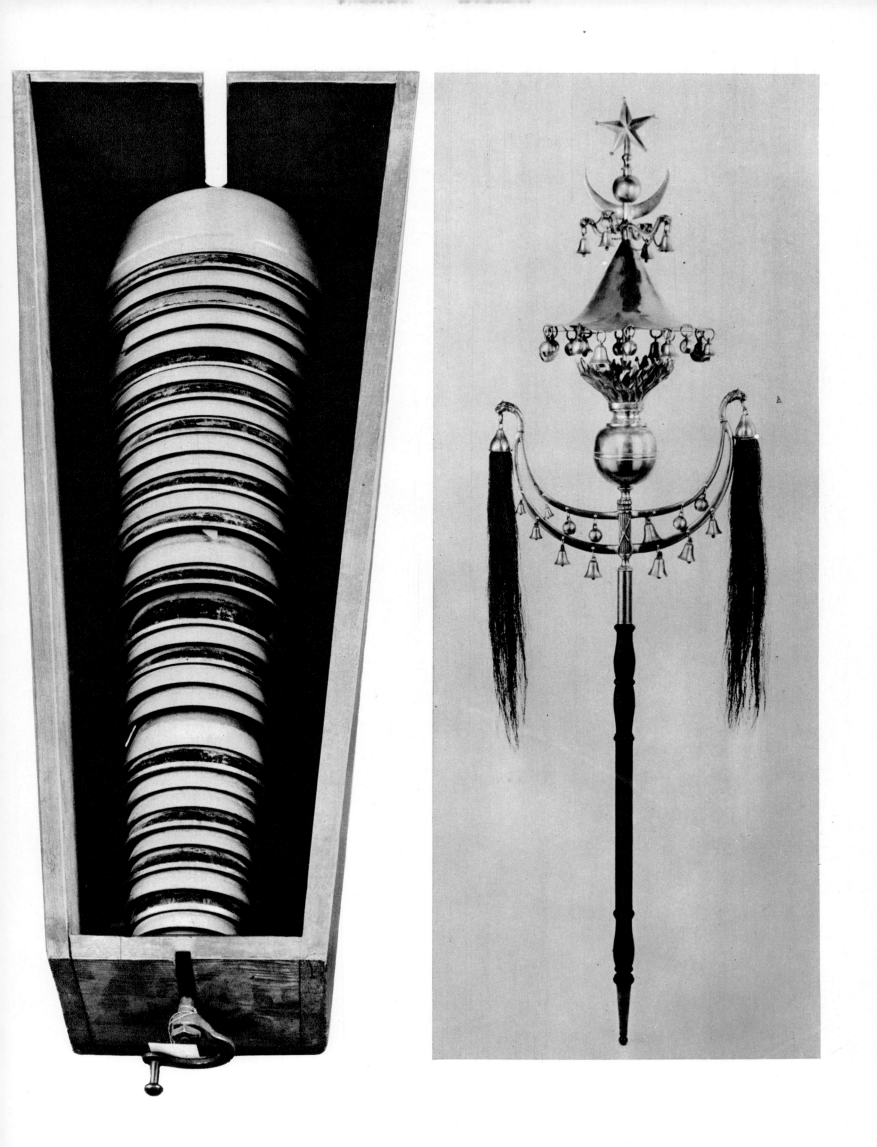

274 Physharmonica, early nineteenth century

275 Portable organ (portative), eighteenth century

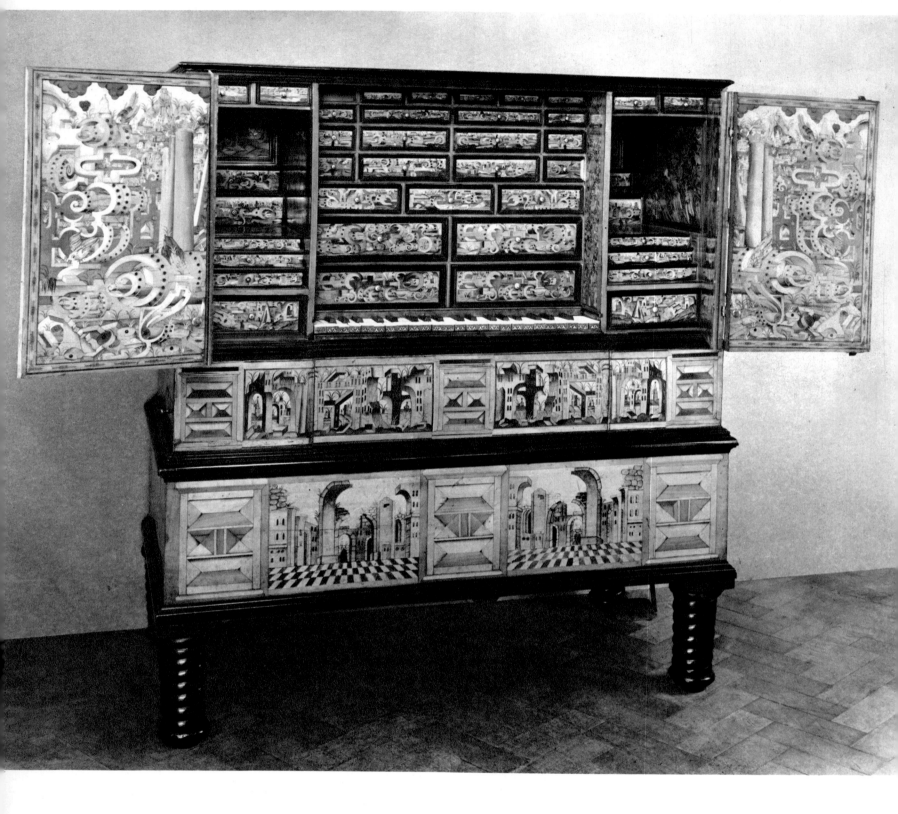

276—7 Chamber organ and detail of the inlaid case, sixteenth century

LAVDATE EVM IN [CH]ORDIS ET ORGAN[IS]

278 Organ in the deanery church in Smečno, Bohemia, 1575
279 Positive made in Bohemia in the eighteenth century

280   Organ of the Týn Church in Prague, built by H. H. Mundr, 1673

281　Organ in the church in Gersfeld, Federal Republic of Germany, made by J. M. Wagner, 1784—7

282—3　Concert organ in the Hall of Antonín Dvořák, Prague

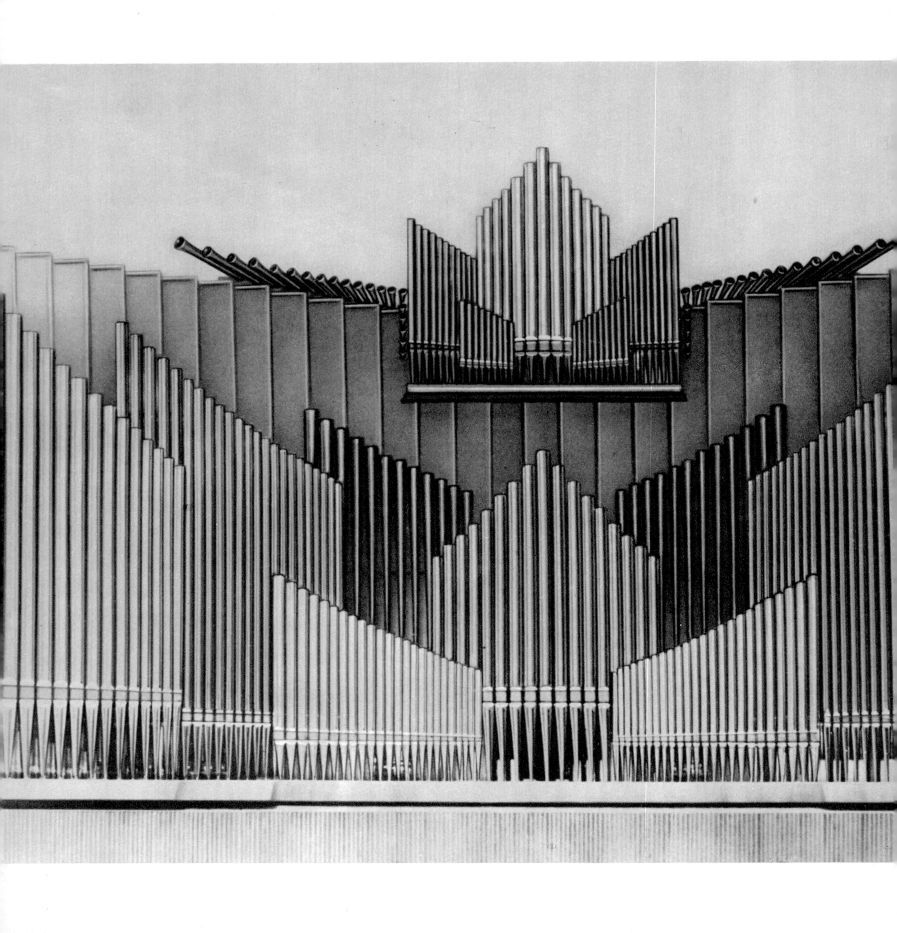

284 Concert organ made in Krnov, Czechoslovakia,
in the broadcasting studio in Bucarest

285—6 Metal flute

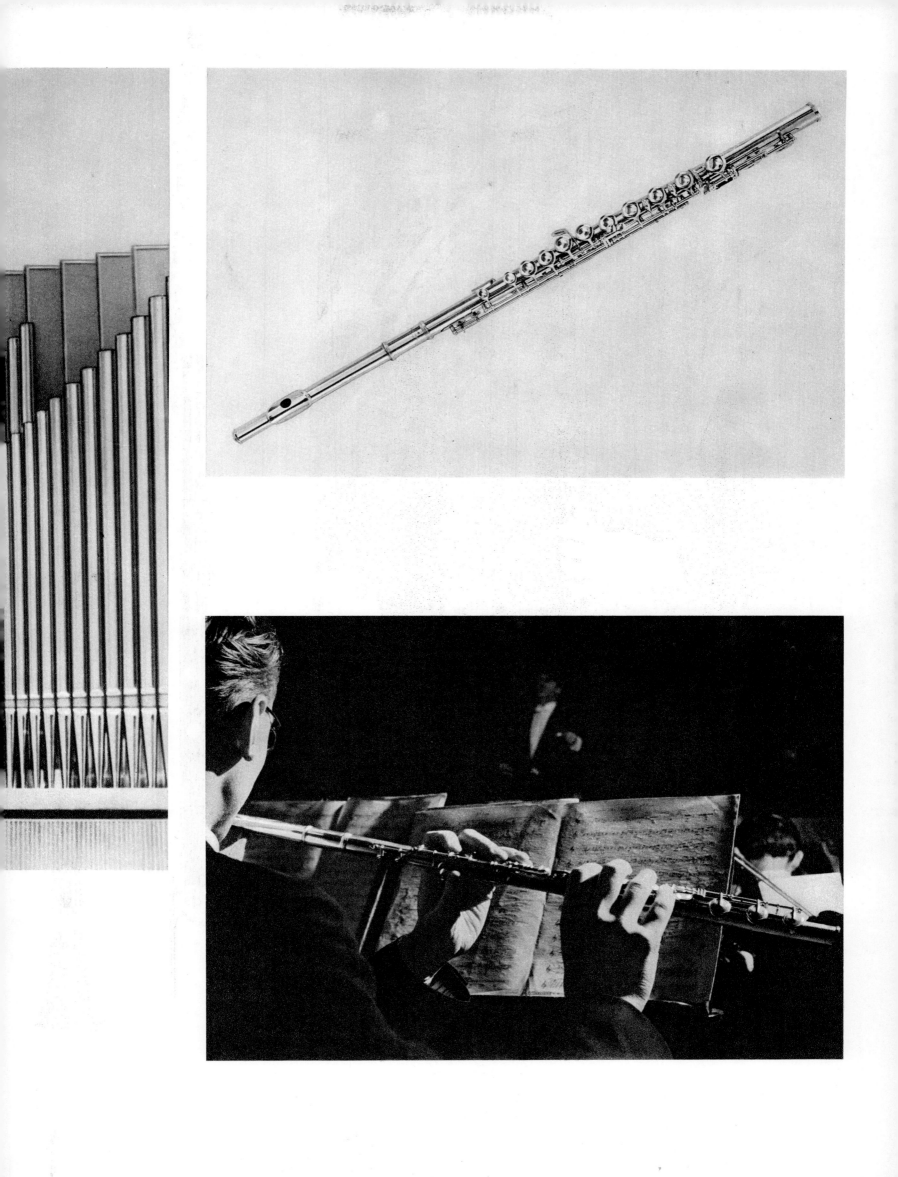

287—9 Bass clarinet and clarinet in B flat

290—2 Oboe and detail of the key mechanism

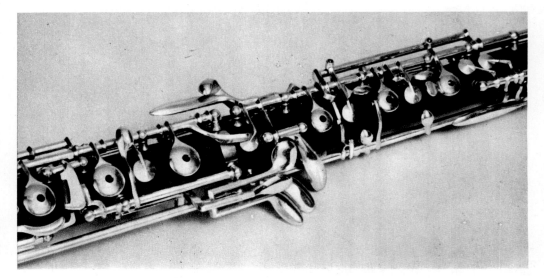

293 Violin made by Antonio Stradivari, played by the virtuoso David Oistrach

294 Masterly play on violoncello

295—6 Bassoon and contra bassoon

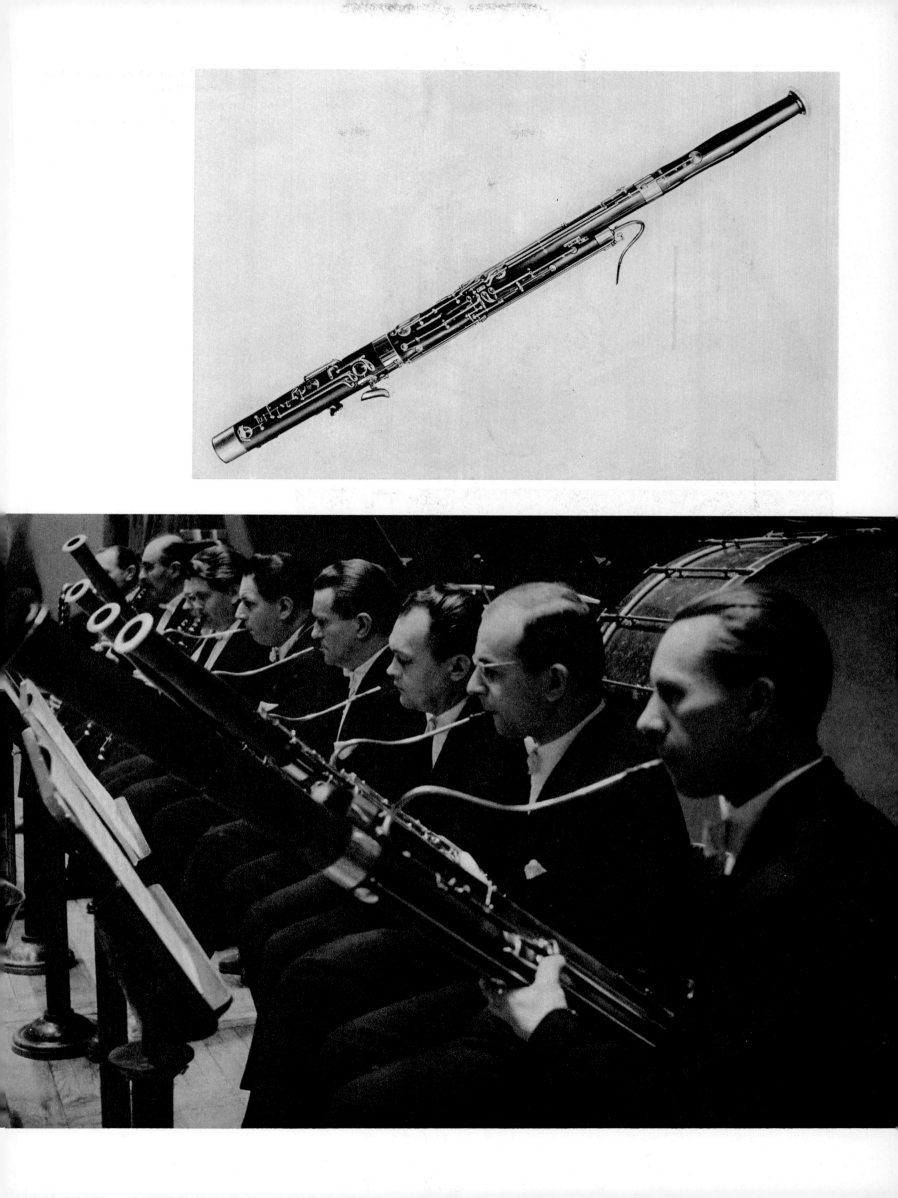

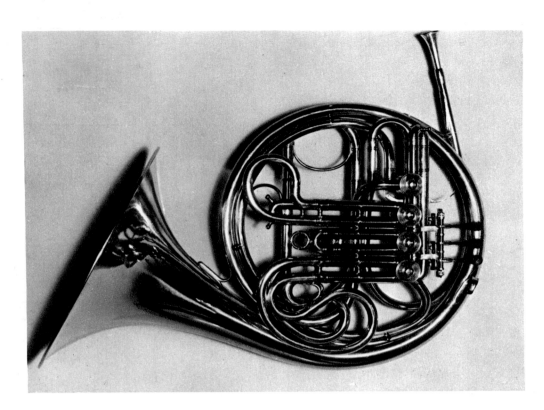

297—8 Double French horn made by Lídl in Brno, Czechoslovakia

299—300 Concert trumpet made in the Amati works in Kraslice, Czechoslovakia

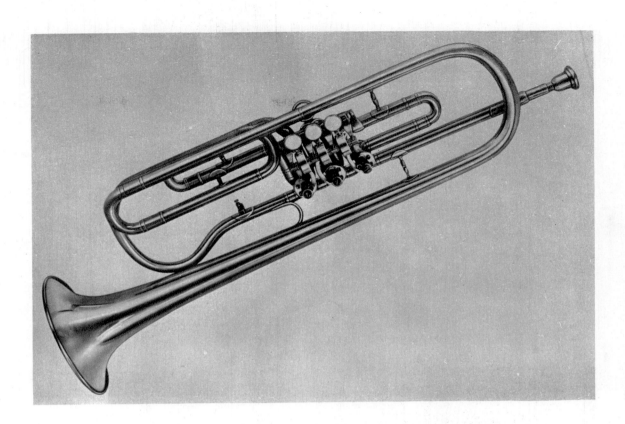

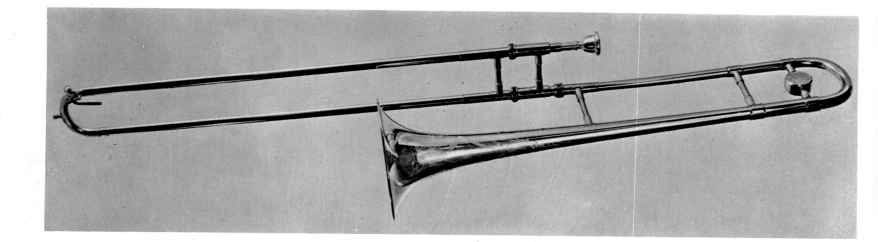

301—2   Slide trombone

303   Tuba in B flat

304   Tuba, model 'Červený', made in the
Amati works, Kraslice, Czechoslovakia

305   Jazz timpani

306   Percussion instruments used in the symphony orchestra: pedal timpani, cymbals, bass drum and tubular bells

307—8   Mouth organs

309   Vibraphone

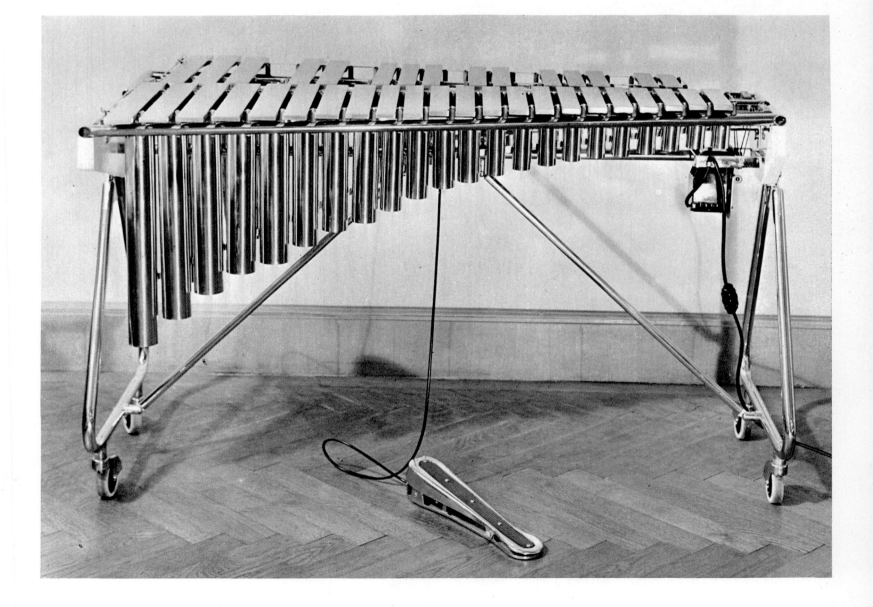

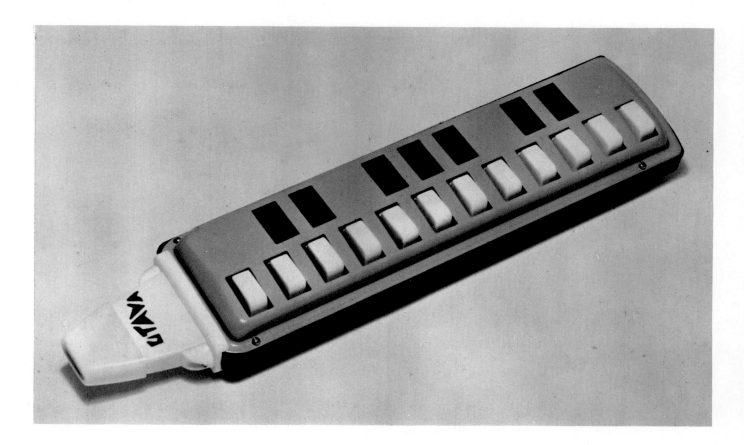

310 Button concertina
311 Piano accordion made in Czechoslovakia
312—13 New types of mouth organs

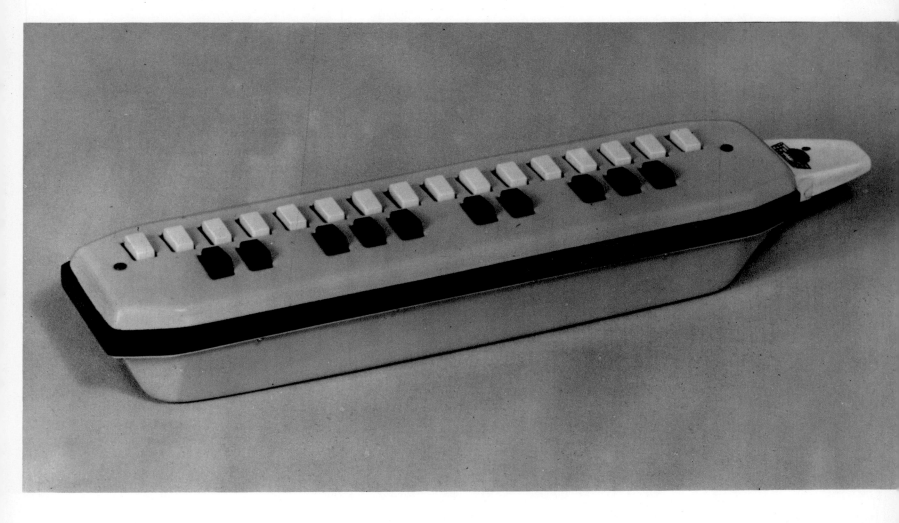

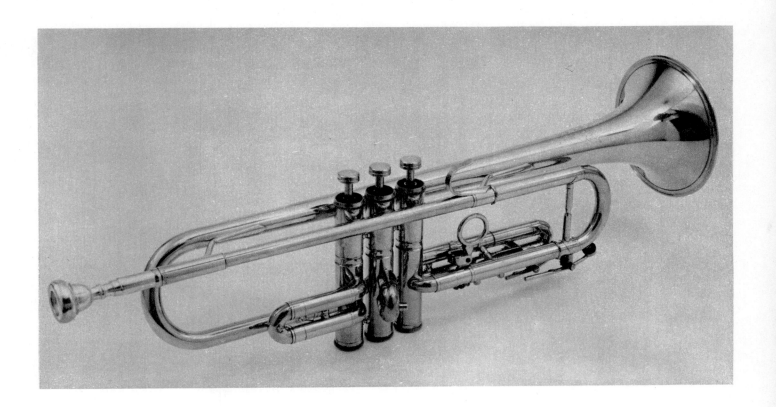

317—18 Jazz trumpet and detail of the valve mechanism

319 Tubon — electronic instrument made
by the J. Mustad works of Göteborg, Sweden

320—1   Electrophonic guitars 'Jolana' of Czechoslovak construction
322   Electronic organ of the 'Eminent 500 Luxe' type
made by the Dutch firm of Vreeken in Bodegraven

323 Electronic musical instrument 'Melodica'
made in the Hohner works in the Federal Republic of Germany

324 Electrophonic dulcimer of French construction

325 Jazz drums

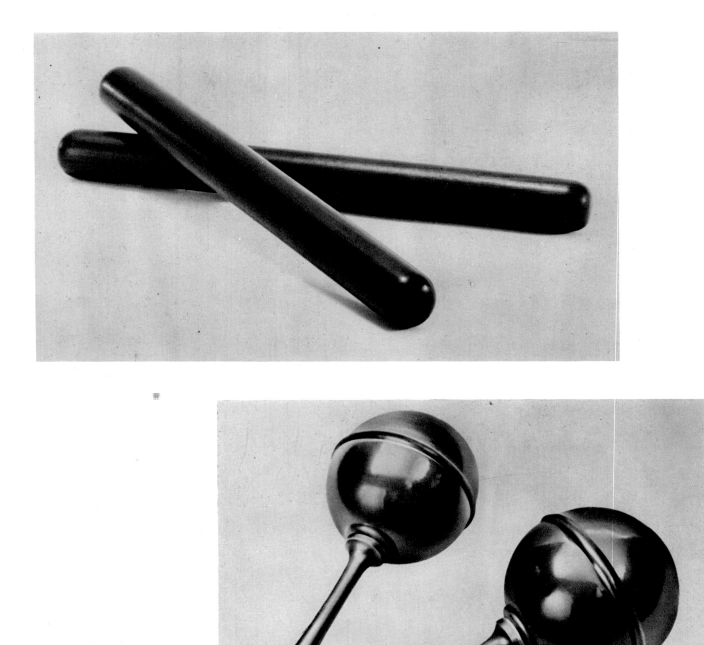
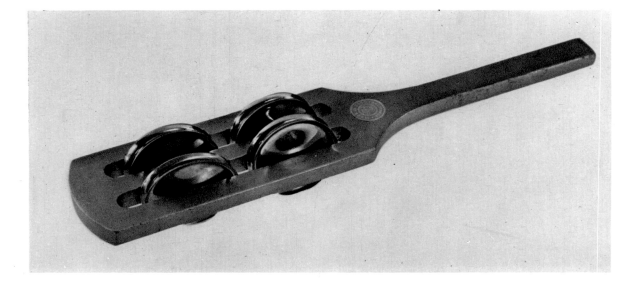

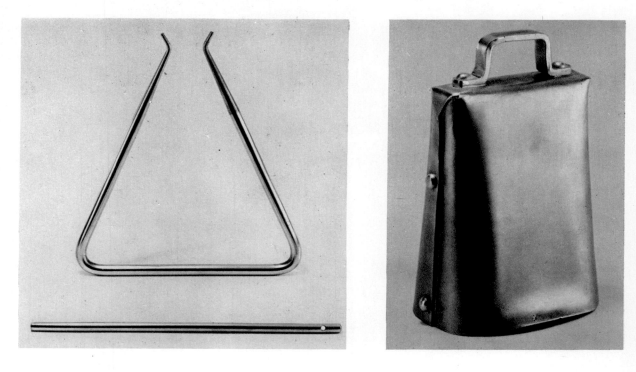

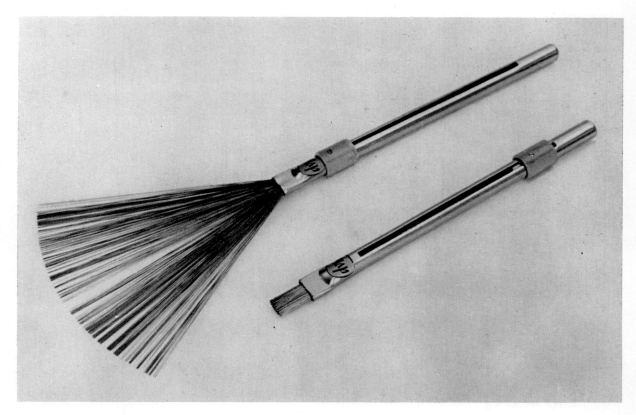

326—31   Jazz instruments: claves, maracas,
mick-pandeira, triangle, cow-bell and wire brushes

332 The concert is over

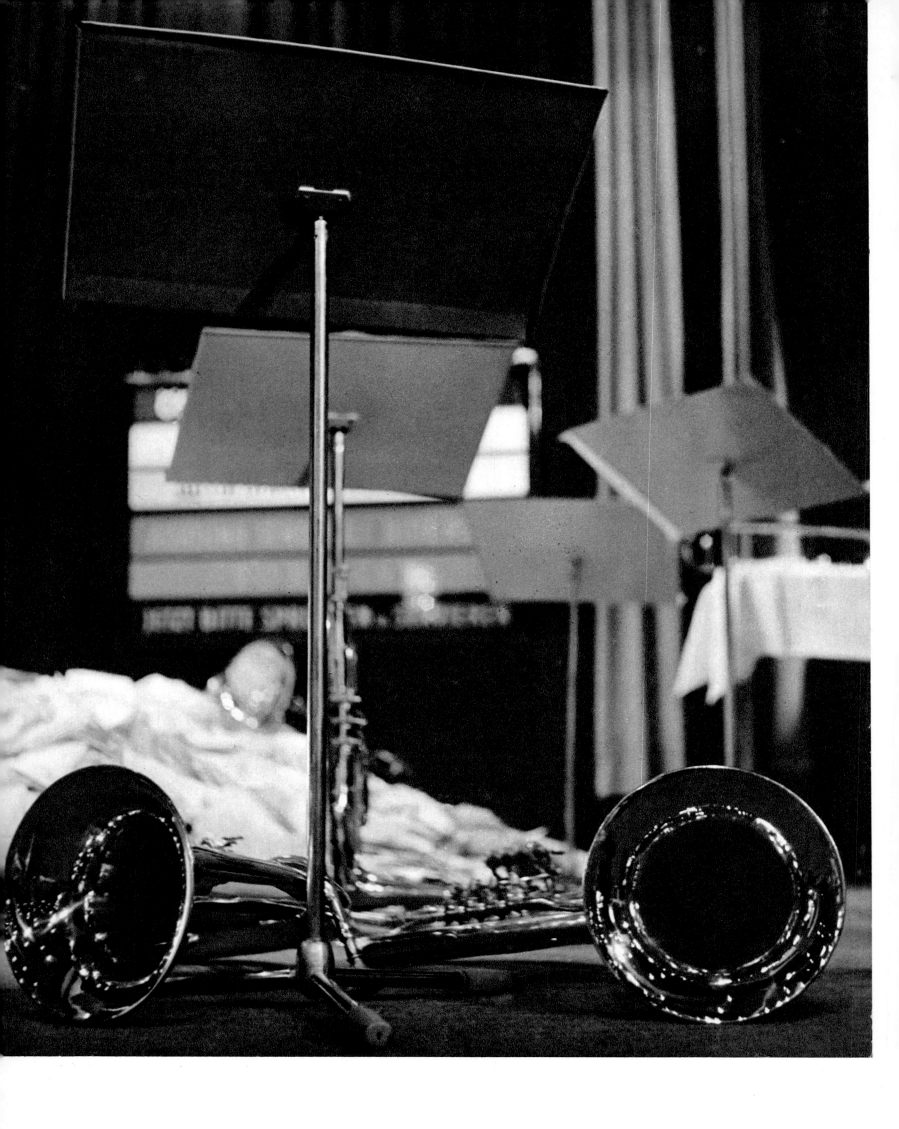

LIST OF PLATES

Pyrenees in 778. In his panic Roland blew the horn so strongly that his neck arteries burst and the horn cracked (Prague, Treasury of St Guy's Cathedral)

40—1 Hunting horn made of elephant tusk and detail of bell; this oliphant was deposited, together with Roland's horn, by Emperor Charles IV at Karlštejn Castle. In the inventory of 1515 both horns are described as having belonged to Roland. From Karlštejn Castle these exquisite instruments found their way to the Treasury of St Guy's Cathedral in Prague; today they are kept at Prague Castle

42 (*Above*) Musical instruments of sacred music — monochord, chimes, organ, harp, Panpipes, cornett
(*Below*) Musical instruments used in secular music — rebec, horn and drum, from the Psalter of Abbot St Remigius of Reims, twelfth century (St John's College, Cambridge)

43 Fiddle; *Mater verborum*, thirteenth century (Prague, National Museum)

44 Crot from the thirteenth-century *Psalterium Juttae Tarsinae* (Monastery Library at Zwettel, Austria)

45 Chimes; *Lectionarium Arnoldi Misnensis* 1290—1300 (Monastery Library at Osek)

46—7 Harp, Bohemian wing (ala bohemica), fiddle and cistra, from the Passional of Abbess Kunhuta, 1319—21 (Prague, University Library)

48—51 Horn, fiddle, trumpet, flute and tabor in the Latin bible known as the Jaroměř Bible, late thirteenth century (Prague, National Museum)

52 Drum and trumpet; miniature in the manuscript *Liber viaticus* of Jan of Středa, second half of the fourteenth century (Prague, National Museum)

53 Minnesinger Heinrich von Frauenlob and musicians with their instruments: drum, flute, shawm, psaltery, two fiddles and bagpipes; illustration from a collection of songs originating in Zurich, the early fourteenth-century Codex of the Manesse family (Heidelberg, University Library)

54—6 Fourteenth-century oliphant and details of its decoration (Prague, National Museum)

57 Psaltery harp, chimes and psaltery, from Velislav's Bible, 1340 (Prague, University Library)

58 Bohemian wing (ala bohemica), cistra, fiddle and psaltery, from Velislav's Bible, 1340 (Prague, University Library)

59 Decachordum (ten-stringed), crot, horn and trumpets from Velislav's Bible, 1340 (Prague, University Library)

60 Psaltery harp from a breviary, 1342 (Monastery Library at Rajhrad)

61 Organ; Bologna breviary, mid-fourteenth century (Prague, University Library)

62 Psaltery harp and flute with tabor and psaltery, Bible of King Wenceslas IV, late fourteenth century (Vienna, State Library)

63 Shawm, trumpets, triangle, organ and fiddle, from the Bible of King Wenceslas IV, late fourteenth century (Vienna, State Library)

64 Latin guitar (guitara latina); detail of a mural painting

Adoration of the Apocalyptic Lamb by Master Theodore of Prague in the Holy Cross Chapel at Karlštejn Castle, c. 1360—70

65 Fiddle; detail of a mural painting at Karlštejn Castle, c. 1360—70

66—8 Bohemian wing (ala bohemica), psaltery and psaltery harp; details of a mural painting at Karlštejn Castle, c. 1360—70

69 Guitara morisca; detail of a mural painting at Karlštejn Castle, c. 1360—70

70 Hand-bells, mandora, fiddle and Bohemian wing (ala Bohemica), from *Six Little Books on Christian Matters* by Tomáš Štítný, c. 1376 (Prague, University Library)

71—2 Lute, shawm and trumpet from the *Krumlov Volume*, early fifteenth century (Prague, National Museum)

73 Horn; mural painting at Karlštejn Castle (Chapel of the Virgin Mary), c. 1360—70

74 Bladder-pipe; mural painting at Karlštejn Castle, c. 1360—70

75—6 Women with mandoras and dancing children with cymbals; marble reliefs on the balustrade of the cantoria in Florence Cathedral by Luca della Robbia c. 1431—8 (Florence, Museo di S. Maria del Fiore)

77 Dulcimer, positive organ, horn, lute, harp, fiddle, flute and tabor, triangle, cross flute, bagpipes; French tapestry, sixteenth century (Boston, Museum of Fine Arts)

78 Fiddle, psaltery, lute, tambourine, portative, clappers, bagpipes, shawm, drums and trumpets, from M. Severinus Boetius: *De Arythmetica, de Musica*, fourteenth century (Naples, National Library)

79 Harp, hurdy-gurdy, psaltery and fiddle from a Calendarium of Irish origin, dating from the end of the thirteenth or the beginning of the fourteenth century (Library of the Křivoklát Castle)

80 Drums, bladder-pipe and organ, from the Lobkovice Breviary, 1494 (Prague, University Library)

81 Pommers and trumpets (one trumpet S-shaped), from the Richenthal Chronicle (known as the *Leningrad Manuscript*) 1464 (Prague, University Library)

82 Clavicytherium: detail of a wooden altar dating from the end of the fifteenth century in the parish church of Kefermarkt, Upper Austria

83 From the left: bells, triangle, recorder, jingles, trumpet, harp, shawm, fiddle, lute, organ, dulcimer, mandora, white (straight) cornett, harp, tromba marina, psaltery, drums, chimes, clavichord, bell and hurdy-gurdy, from Otto von Passau: *Codex*, c. 1448 (Coburg, library of the Casimir School)

84 Drums, fiddle, horn, triangle, lute and bagpipes, from the Olomouc Bible, 1417 (Olomouc, University Library)

85 Violas da gamba and da braccio, by Matthias Grünewald (c. 1470—83 — c. 1510), from the Isenheim Altar (Colmar Museum)

86—7 Psaltery and lute, lyre and rebec, from marble

134 Organ, flute, violin and violoncello: painting on a goblet made in Bohemia, mid-eighteenth century (Prague, Museum of Industrial Arts)

135 Harp and French horns: painting on a goblet made in Bohemia, mid-eighteenth century (Prague, Museum of Industrial Arts)

136 French horn, zither and timpani: engraving on a goblet made in Bohemia, c. 1700 (Prague, Museum of Industrial Arts)

137 Bassoon and French horn: Viennese porcelain, eighteenth century (Prague, Museum of Industrial Arts)

138 Lira da gamba by Pier Francesco Mola (1612—68) (Dresden Gallery)

139 *Playing Women,* showing tenor viola da gamba, organ, cross flute, psaltery, lira da braccio, by Tintoretto (1518—94) (Dresden Gallery)

140 *Madonna with St Jerome and St Laurencius* showing viola da gamba and lute, by Francesco Francia, 1500 (Leningrad, Hermitage)

141 *Muses,* showing bass viola da gamba, by Eustache Lesueur (1617—55) (Paris, Louvre)

142 Seventeenth-century dulcimer (Milan, Castello Sforzesco)

143 Seventeenth-century dulcimer (London, Horniman Museum)

144—5 Sixteenth-century soprano lute (Milan, Castello Sforzesco)

146 Lute made by Georg Gerle in Innsbruck, c. 1580 (Vienna, Kunsthistorisches Museum)

147 Lute made by Hans Frey in Bologna, end of the sixteenth century (Vienna, Kunsthistorisches Museum)

148 *Concert,* depicting fiddle, recorder and lute, by Ercole de Roberti (c. 1450—96) (London, National Gallery)

149—50 Lute and violin, detail of painting by Michelangelo da Caravaggio (c. 1560—1609) (Leningrad, Hermitage)

151—2 Theorbo made by the lute- and violin-maker Martin Brunner in Olomouc and detail of the pegbox, 1764 (Prague, National Museum)

153 Theorbo-lute by Ferdinand Bol (1616—80) (Stockholm, National Museum)

154 *Portrait of Françoise Leijoncrone,* showing a lute, by Michael Dahl, c. 1700 (Stockholm, National Museum)

155—6 Lute made by Max Unverdorben in Venice and detail of the rose, sixteenth century (Prague, National Museum)

157—8 Lute made by Tomáš Edlinger in Prague and detail of the rose, late seventeenth century (Prague, National Museum)

159—60 Italian theorbo-lute, seventeenth century (London, Horniman Museum)

161 *The Music Lesson,* with a theorbo-lute by Frans van Mieris (1635—81) (Dresden Gallery)

162 Chitarrone (archlute) made by the Spanish instrument-maker Johannes Mantoya de Cardone, 1591 (London, Horniman Museum)

163—4 Chitarrone and detail of roses, made by the Prague violin-maker Karel B. Dvořák at the end of the nineteenth century, after the original instrument made by Martin Schott in Prague in 1680, which is now in the Louvre (Prague, National Museum)

165—6 Pandurine with detail of the rose, Italian work, 1673 (London, Horniman Museum)

167—8 Mandora made by the violin-maker Michael Angiolo Bergonzi of Cremona and detail of the scroll, 1765 (London, Horniman Museum)

169 Neapolitan mandoline made by Johann Jobst Franck in Dresden, 1789 (Prague, National Museum)

170 Milanese mandoline (mandora) made by Francesco Plesber in Milan, 1773 (Prague, National Museum)

171 Eighteenth-century Italian mandoline (London, Horniman Museum)

172 Cittern made by Girolamo de Virchi in Brescia for Archduke Ferdinand of Tyrol, 1574 (Vienna, Kunsthistorisches Museum)

173 Arch-cittern in lyre form, sixteenth or seventeenth century (Vienna, Kunsthistorisches Museum)

174—5 Bell-cittern (Hamburg cittern), probably by the Hamburg violin-maker Joachim Tielke, c. 1700 (London, Victoria and Albert Museum)

176 *Cittern player,* by Giacomo Francesco Cipper (Tedesco), eighteenth century (Stockholm, National Museum)

177 Cistra made by Maxmilian Zacher in Breslau, 1751 (Prague, National Museum)

178 Guitar-cittern (English guitar) made by Jan Michael Willer in Prague, 1799 (Prague, National Museum)

179 Guitar made by the Venice instrument-maker Georgius Sellas, first half of the seventeenth century (Prague, National Museum)

180 Guitar made by the Prague violin-maker Tomáš Ondřej Hulinzký, 1754 (Prague, National Museum)

181 Back of a guitar made by G. Sellas (Prague, National Museum)

182 Plectrum guitar (chitarra battente) with an inscription reading: *Vincentius Vinaccio filius Januarii fecit Neapoli alla Rua Catalana A. D. 1772* (London, Horniman Museum)

183 Detail of a guitar made by J. Tielke (see plates 184—5)

184—5 Guitar made by Joachim Tielke in Hamburg, late seventeenth century (London, Horniman Museum)

186 Detail of *Gay Party,* with guitar, cross flute and lute, by Jan Massys, sixteenth century (Stockholm, National Museum)

187—8 Italian chitarra battente, seventeenth century (London, Horniman Museum)

189–90   Guitar made by the lute-maker Matthias Fux in Vienna and detail of the sunken rose, 1692 (Prague, National Museum)

191–2   Arpanetta made in Germany and detail of the rose, seventeenth century (London, Horniman Museum)

193–4   Guitar made by the Portuguese instrument-maker José Pereira-Coelho, 1800 (London, Horniman Museum)

195   Nineteenth-century guitar, modified by Ritter and equipped with two capotastos for the basic chords of varying pitch; the tuning of the twenty-four wire strings is indicated by notes on the soundboard of the instrument (London, Horniman Museum)

196   Nineteenth-century dital harp, invented by the Englishman Light; the instrument is equipped on the reverse with ditals, which have the same function as pedals on a harp (London, Horniman Museum)

197–9   Pedal harp built by H. Nadermann in Paris and details, 1785 (London, Victoria and Albert Museum)

200   Pedal harp with hook action, from a colour engraving of St Cecilia, late eighteenth century (Prague, National Museum)

201–2   Modern pedal harp built by Alois Červenka in Prague, and detail of another harp by the same maker

203   Marie Antoinette's 'golden harp' made by Cousineau Père et Fils in Paris, late eighteenth century (Budapest, National Museum)

204–6   Virginal belonging to Catherine of Brandenburg and details of the instrument, c. 1620–30 (Budapest, National Museum)

207   Ottavina spinet, seventeenth century (London, Horniman Museum)

208   Harpsichord made by Vitus de Trasuntinus in Venice, 1560 (Berlin, State Institute for Music)

209–10   Miniature virginal and detail, 1575 (London, Horniman Museum)

211   Lady at the clavichord, from an engraving by Václav Hollar, 1635 (Prague, National Gallery)

212   Fretted clavichord made in Holland, seventeenth century (Berlin, State Institute for Music)

213   Harpsichord made by Joannes Gorman in Paris, 1738 (Stockholm, Museum of Musical History)

214   Square piano built by Leopold Sauer in Prague, early nineteenth century (Prague, City Museum)

215   Two-manual harpsichord built by Pietro Todino in Milan, 1675 (Milan, Museum of Musical Instruments, Castello Sforzesco)

216   Double-manual harpsichord combined with spinet by Johannes Ruckers, Antwerp, 1619 (Brussels, Museum of Musical Instruments at the Royal Academy of Music)

217   Harpsichord with the keyboard made of mother-of pearl and tortoise-shell, seventeenth century (Prague, National Museum)

218   The earliest double virginal made by Johannes Ruckers in Antwerp, 1581 (New York, Metropolitan Museum of Art)

219   Lutes, shawms, flutes, from a detail of the painting of the double virginal in plate 218 (New York, Metropolitan Museum of Art)

220   Harpsichord, seventeenth century (Treviso, Museo Civico — L. Bailo)

221   Piano, eighteenth century (Treviso, Museo Civico — L. Bailo)

222   Two-manual harpsichord of Joseph Haydn made by Burkat Shudi et Johannes Broadwood in London, 1775 (Vienna, Kunsthistorisches Museum; collections of the Association of the Friends of Music)

223   Forte piano, eighteenth century; Mozart played this instrument when he was in Prague in January 1787 (Prague, National Museum, Bertramka Mansion)

224   Pyramid piano with a clock made by the Prague piano-maker Leopold Sauer, early nineteenth century (Prague, City Museum)

225   Clavicytherium (upright harpsichord); it was built for Emperor Leopold I by Martinus Kaiser, mid-seventeenth century (Vienna, Kunsthistorisches Museum)

226   Giraffe piano made in Bohemia, first half of the nineteenth century (Prague, National Museum)

227   Piano made by Johann Baptista Streicher in Vienna; Liszt played this instrument during his visit to Prague in 1846 (Prague, National Museum)

228   Clavichord made by Arnold Dolmetsch, 1894 (Milan, Museum of Musical Instruments, Castello Sforzesco)

229   Square piano with pedal-board made by Gaetano Scappa in Milan, 1804 (Milan, Museum of Musical Instruments, Castello Sforzesco)

230   *Flute, lute and bumbass;* painting by Jan Steen (1626–79) (Prague, National Gallery)

231   Fiddle: detail from painting of St John (c. 1504) (Cracow, National Museum)

232   Lira da braccio made by Joannes Andrea, Verona, 1511 (Vienna, Kunsthistorisches Museum)

233   Lira da braccio: detail from the fresco *Parnassus* by Raffaello Santi (1483–1520) (Vatican)

234   Viola da braccio: painting by an anonymous sixteenth-century painter (Rome, Doria Gallery)

235   Violoncello, lute and violin: gingerbread mould, late seventeenth century (Kuks, Bohemia, Czechoslovakia)

236–8   Three gambas made by the Brescian violin-maker Gasparo da Salò, second half of the sixteenth century (Vienna, Kunsthistorisches Museum)

239–40   Viola d'amore made by the violin-maker Andreas N. Bartl in Vienna, second half of the eighteenth century (Private collection)

241–2   Viola d'amore and English violetta made by the

LIST OF ILLUSTRATIONS IN THE TEXT

ACKNOWLEDGEMENTS

Acknowledgement is made to the following individuals and institutions who have kindly supplied photographs

Anderson, Rome: *92, 93, 104, 148, 233, 234*
Appeltofft B., Stockholm: *319*
Arkeoloji Müzesi, Ankara: *12*

British Museum, London: *19, 22, 23*
Brok J., Prague: *134, 135, 137*
Brückner, Coburg: *83*
Buchner A., Prague: *4, 6, 7, 8, 11, 13, 16—18, 20, 26, 32, 38, 42, 43, 48—54, 57, 58, 60, 61, 70, 73, 74, 79, 110, 111, 116, 117, 126, 131—3, 143, 159, 160, 162, 165—8, 171, 182, 183—5, 187, 188, 191—6, 201, 202, 207, 209—11, 214, 224, 227, 239, 240, 250—6, 267—9, 272, 278*

Conservatoire Royal de Musique — Musée Instrumental, Brussels: *216*
Československá tisková kancelář (Czechoslovak Press Agency), Prague: *321*
Chochola V., Prague: *287, 290, 296, 306*

Deutsche Fotothek, Dresden: *138, 139, 161*
Dingjan A., The Hague: *124*

Encyclopédie Photographique de l'Art, Paris: *15*

Frank M., Prague: *304, 332*
Fratelli Fabbri, Milan: *78*

Hermitage, Leningrad: *109, 140, 149, 150*
Hevr A., Prague: *84*
Hickmann H., Cairo: *24, 25*
Hirmer, Munich: *27*
Honty T., Prague: *10, 39—41, 55, 56, 226*

Illek F. and Paul A., Prague: *80*

Kolowca S., Cracow: *105, 106, 231, 260*
Krahulec J., Prague: *179, 180, 217, 223, 243, 247, 248, 271, 274, 275, 279*
Kunsthistorisches Museum — Sammlung alter Musikinstrumente, Vienna: *125, 146, 147, 172, 173, 222, 225, 231, 236—8, 244, 245*

Landesgewerbeamt, Baden-Württemberg: *323*
Lukas J., Prague: *286, 302, 308*

Magyar Nemzeti Múzeum, Budapest: *203—6*
Malard J., Paris: *324*
Martínek F., Prague: *282, 283*

Metropolitan Museum of Art, New York: *218, 219*
Moravian Museum, Brno: *1—3, 5*
Moretti, Rimini: *86, 87*
Müller E., Kassel: *85, 130, 280, 281*
Musée du Louvre, Paris: *21*
Museo Civico — L. Bailo, Treviso: *220, 221*
Museo Nazionale, Naples: *29, 34—7*
Museo Nazionale, Ravenna: *30*
Museum muzykalnych instrumentov, Leningrad: *257*
Museum of Fine Arts, Boston: *77*
Musical Instruments (Hipkins), Edinburgh: *123*
Musikhistoriska Museet, Stockholm: *213*

National Gallery, Prague: *97, 121*
National Museum, Prague: *104*
Nationalmuseet, Copenhagen: *9*
Nationalmuseet, Stockholm: *119, 153, 154, 176, 186, 246*
Nationalmuseu, Bucarest: *31*
Neruda J., Prague: *181, 200*

Peterka M., Prague: *293*
Publifoto, Milan: *142, 144, 145, 229*

Rapid, Prague: *99, 108, 112—15, 151, 152, 155—8, 163, 164, 169, 170, 177, 178, 189, 190. 241, 242, 259, 261—7, 273, 284, 285, 288, 289, 291, 292, 294, 295, 297—9, 301, 303, 305, 307, 309—15, 317, 318, 320, 325—31*
Renner B., Prague: *96, 100*
Revue d'Assyriologie, Paris: *14*
Rosegnal V., Prague: *300*

Saporetti, Milan: *215, 228*
Staatliches Institut für Musikforschung — Musikinstrumen-ten-Museum, Berlin: *92, 208, 212*
Státní ústav památkové péče a ochrany přírody (State Institute for Protection of Monuments and Nature), Prague: *44, 45, 59, 62—9, 71, 72, 81, 82, 90, 91, 94, 120, 122, 127, 128, 258, 270*
Štenc, Prague: *28, 75, 76, 88, 89, 107, 118, 129, 136, 141, 230, 249*

University Library, Prague: *46, 47*

Victoria and Albert Museum, London: *101—3, 174, 175, 197—9, 276*
Vreeken, Bodegraven: *322*

Wadsworth Atheneum, Hartford: *95*

BIBLIOGRAPHY

Adlung J., *Gründlicher Unterricht von der Struktur, Gebrauch und Erhaltung. Ec. der Orgeln, Clavicymbel, Clavichordien und anderer Instrumente*, 2 vols, Berlin, 1768; facsimile edition, Kassel, 1966

van Aerde R., *Les Tuerlinckx*, Luthiers à Malines, Malines, 1914

Agricola M., *Musica instrumentalis deudsch*. Wittenberg, 1528 and 1545; facsimile edition, Leipzig, 1896

Albini E., *Instrumenti musicali degli Etruschi e loro origini*, L'illustrazione Vaticana, 1937

Altenburg J. E., *Versuch einer Anleitung zur heroisch-musikalischen Trompeter- und Paukert-Kunst*, Halle, 1795; facsimile edition, Leipzig, 1911

Altenburg W., *Die Klarinette*, Heilbronn, 1904

Alton R., *Violin and Cello*, London, 1964

Andersson O., *The Bowed-Harp: A Study in the History of Early Musical Instruments*, London, 1930

Andries J., *Aperçu théorique de tous les Instruments de Musique, actuellement en usage*, Ghent, 1856

Apian-Bennewitz P. O., *Die Geige, der Geigenbau und die Bogenverfertigung*, Weimar, 1892

Arakelian S., *Die Geige*, Frankfurt, 1968

Armstrong R. B., *Musical Instruments, Part I: The Irish and the Highland Harps*, Edinburgh, 1904; *Part III: English and Irish Instruments*, 1908

Arnaut de Zwolle, *Instruments de Musique du XVe siècle*, Paris, n. d.

Asriel A., *Jazz*, Berlin, 1966

Audsley G. A., *The Art of Organ Building*, New York, 1905; *The Organ of the Twentieth Century . . .*, New York, 1919

Avgerinos G., *Lexikon der Pauke*, Frankfurt, 1964; *Handbuch der Schlag- und Effektinstrumente*, Frankfurt, 1967

Aznar y García F., *Indumentaria española . . .*, Madrid, 1880

Bahnert-Herzberg-Schramm, *Metallblasinstrumente*, Leipzig, 1958

Bacher J., *Die Viola da Gamba*, Kassel, 1932

Bachmann A., *Le Violon*, Paris, 1906

Bachmann W., *Die Anfänge des Streichinstrumentenspiels*, Leipzig, 1964

Baines A., *Woodwind Instruments and their History*, London, 1957; *Musical Instruments through the Ages*, London, 1963; *European and American Musical Instruments*, London, 1966; *Victoria and Albert Museum, Catalogue of Musical Instruments, II: Non-Keyboard Instruments*, London, 1968

Balfoort D. J., *Eigenartige Musikinstrumente*, The Hague, n. d.

Balfour H., *The Natural History of the Musical Bow*, Oxford, 1899

Banach J., *Tematy muzyczne w plastyce polskiej*, Cracow, 1956

Baron E. G., *Historisch-theoretische und praktische Untersuchung des Instruments der Lauten*, Nuremberg, 1727; facsimile edition, Amsterdam, 1965

Bartl F. K., *Abhandlung von der Tastenharmonika*, Brno, 1798

Bate P., *The Oboe*, London, 1956; *The Trumpet and Trombone*, London, 1966

Bechler L. and Rahm B., *Die Oboe und die ihr verwandten Instrumente . . .*, Leipzig, 1914

Bedbrook G. S., *Keyboard Music from the Middle Ages*, London, 1949

Bedos de Celles F., *L'Art du Facteur d'Orgues*, Paris, 1776, 2 vols; facsimile edition, Kassel, 1934

Behn F., *Musikleben im Altertum und frühen Mittelalter*, Stuttgart, 1954

Bemetzrieder A., *Leçons de Clavecin et Principes d'Harmonie*, Paris, 1771; facsimile edition, Paris, 1966

Berendt J. E., *Das neue Jazzbuch*, Frankfurt, 1959

Bermudo J., *Declaración de Instrumentos musicales*, Ossuna, 1955; facsimile edition, Kassel, 1957

Berr A., *Geigen: Originale, Kopien, Fälschungen, Verfälschungen*, Frankfurt, 1967

Bessaraboff N., *Ancient European Musical Instruments*, Boston, 1941

Besseler H., *Die Musik des Mittelalters und der Renaissance*, Potsdam, 1931

Beyer R., *Elektronische Musik*, Melos, February 1954

Bianchini F., *De Tribus Generibus Instrumentorum Musicae Veterum Organicae Dissertatio*, Rome, 1742

Bierdimpfl K. A., *Bayerisches Nationalmuseum, Catalogue*, Munich 1883

Boalch D., *Makers of the Harpsichord and Clavichord*, London, 1956

Boehm T., *Die Flöte und das Flötenspiel . . .*, Munich, 1871

Bonanni F., *Gabinetto armonico pieno d'istrumenti sonori indicati . . .*, Rome, 1722; facsimile edition, Kassel, 1965

Bonhard V. and Prach J., *Piana a pianina (Pianos and Upright Pianos)*, Prague, 1958

Borjon C. E., *Traité de musette*, Lyons, 1672

Bornefeld H., *Das Positiv*, Kassel, 1941

Boston C. N. and Langwill L. G., *Church and Chamber Barrel-Organs*, Edinburgh, 1967

Bottée de Toulmon A., *Dissertation sur les instruments de musique employés au Moyen Age*, Paris, 1844

Bouasse H., *Tuyaux et résonateurs. Introduction à l'étude des instruments à vent*, Paris, 1929; *Instruments à vent, I: Anches métalliques et membraneuses. Tuyaux à anche et à bouche. Orgues. Instruments à embouchure de cor*, Paris, 1929; *II: Instruments à piston, à anche, à embouchure de flûte*, Paris, 1930; *Cordes et membranes. Instruments de musique à cordes et à membranes*, Paris, 1926

Boyden D., *The History of Violin Playing*, London, 1965

Bragard R. and De Hen F. J., *Les instruments de musique dans l'art et l'histoire*, Rhode-St-Genèse, 1967

Brancour R., *Histoire des instruments de musique . . .*, Paris, 1921

Brandimeier J., *Handbuch der Zither*, Munich, 1963

Bricqueville E., *Un coin de la curiosité. Les anciens instruments de musique*, Paris, 1894; *Les musettes*, Paris, 1894; *Notice sur la vielle*, Paris, 1911; *Les vents d'instruments de musique au XVIIIe siècle*, Paris, 1908; *La viole d'amour*, Paris, 1908

Broholm H., Larsen W. and Skjerne G., *The Lurs of the Bronze Age*, Copenhagen, 1949

Buck P., *Die Gitarre und ihre Meister*, Berlin, 1926

Buhle E., *Die Musikalischen Instrumente in den Miniaturen des frühen Mittelalters, 1. Die Blasinstrumente*, Leipzig, 1903; *Verzeichnis der Sammlung alter Musikinstrumente im Bachhause zu Eisenach*, Leipzig, 1919

Buchner A., *Průvodce výstavou České hudebni nástroje minulosti (Exposition guide: Czech Musical Instruments of the Past)*, Prague, 1950; *Zaniklé dřevěné dechové nástroje 16. stoleti (Extinct woodwind instruments of the sixteenth century)*, Prague, 1952; *Hudebni nástroje od pravěku k dnešku (Musical Instruments throughout the Ages)*, Prague, 1956; *České automatofony (Czech automatophones)*, Prague, 1957; *Hudebni automaty (Musical automats)*, Prague, 1958; *Průvodce výstavou České hudebni nástroje v Nelahozevsi (Exposition guide — Czech Musical Instruments in Nelahozeves)*, Prague, 1959; *Hudouci andělé na Karlštejně (Fiddling Angels at Karlštejn Castle)*, Prague, 1967; *Hudebni nástroje národů (Musical Instruments of the World)*, Prague, 1969

Burian E. F., *Jazz*, Prague, 1928

Cabos, F., *Le violon et la lutherie*, Paris, 1947

Carse A., *Musical Wind Instruments . . .*, London, 1939; *Catalogue of the Adam Carse Collection of Old Musical Wind Instruments*, London, 1951

Cerone D. P., *El Melopeo y Maestro*, Naples, 1613

Cerreto S., *Della prattica musica vocale et instrumentale . . .*, Naples, 1601

Cervelli L., *Contributi alla storia degli strumenti musicali in Italia. Rinascimento e Barocco*, Rome, 1967

Chailley J., *La Musique médiévale*, Paris, 1951

Chouquet G., *Le Musée du Conservatoire National de Musique. Catalogue descriptif et raisonné*, Paris, 1903

Clappé A. A., *The Wind-Band and its Instruments*, New York, 1911

Claudius C., *Samling af Gamle Musikinstrumenter*, Copenhagen, 1931

Closson E., *Histoire du piano*, Brussels, 1944

Comettant O., *Histoire d'un Inventeur du XIXᵉ siècle (A. Sax)*, Paris, 1860; *La Musique, les Musiciens et les Instruments de Musique*, Paris, 1869

Coussemaker E., *Mémoire sur Hucbald ... et sur les instruments de musique*, Paris, 1841

Coutagne H., *Gaspard Duiffoproucart et les luthiers du XVIᵉ siècle*, Paris, 1893

Daubeny U., *Orchestral Wind Instruments, Ancient and Modern*, London, 1920

Dauer A. M., *Jazz, die magische Musik*, Bremen, 1961

Davis B., *The Saxophone*, London, n. d.

Day C. R., *Descriptive Catalogue of the Musical Instruments in the Royal Military Exhibition of 1890*, London, 1891

Denis J., *Traité de l'Accord de l'Espinette*, 1650, facsimile edition, Kassel, 1968

Denis V., *De Muziekinstrumenten in de Nederlanden en in Italie naar hun Afbeelding in de XVᵉ eeuwsche Kunst*, Antwerp, 1944

De Picolellis G., *Liutai antichi e moderni*, Florence, 1855

Dolmetsch A., *Dolmetsch and his Instruments. Evolution of the Dolmetsch Instruments*, Surrey, 1929

Dolmetsch N., *The Viola da Gamba*, London, 1962

Dorf R., *Electronic Musical Instruments*, New York, 1954

Doring E., *The Guadagnini Family of Violinmakers*, Chicago, 1949

Douglas A., *The Electronic Music Instrument Manual*, London, 1957

Dräger H. H., *Die Entwicklung des Streichbogens und seine Anwendung in Europa bis zum Violenbogen des 16. Jahrhunderts*, Berlin, 1937

Dufourcq N., *Documents inédits relatifs à l'Orgue français*, 2 vols, Paris, 1934—5; *Esquisse d'une Histoire de l'Orgue en France du XIIIᵉ au XVIIIᵉ siècle*, Paris, 1935

Dyson Sir G., *Catalogue of Historical Musical Instruments, Paintings, Sculptures and Drawings*, London, 1952

Eichborn H., *Die Trompete in alter und neuer Zeit*, Leipzig, 1881; *Das alte Clarinblasen auf Trompeten*, Leipzig, 1894; *Die Dämpfung beim Horn*, Leipzig, 1897

Eichelberger H. et al., *Das Akkordeon*, Leipzig, 1964

Eimert H., *Information über serielle Musik. I. Elektronische Musik*, Vienna, 1955

Einstein A., *Music in the Romantic Era*, New York, 1947

Eisel J. T., *Musicus autodidactus*, Erfurt, 1738

Elgar R., *Introduction to the Double Bass*, St Leonards-on-Sea, 1960; *More about the Double Bass*, St Leonards-on-Sea, 1960

Ellerhorst W., *Handbuch der Orgelkunde*, Einsiedeln, 1936

Ellis A. J., *The History of Musical Pitch*, London, 1880

Emsheimer E., *Musikhistoriska Museet*, Stockholm, 1955

Engel C., *A Descriptive Catalogue of the Musical Instruments in the South Kensington Museum*, London, 1874; *Researches into the Early History of the Violin Family*, London, 1883

Eppelsheim J., *Das Orchester des Lully*, Tutzing, 1961

Epstein P., *Historisches Museum Frankfurt a/M. Sammlung alter Musikinstrumente*, Frankfurt, 1927

Euting E., *Zur Geschichte der Blasinstrumente im 16. und 17. Jahrhundert*, Berlin, 1899

Exposição internacional de instrumentos antigos, Lisbon, 1961

Farga F., *Geigen und Geiger*, Zürich, 1940

Farmer H. G., *The Organ of the Ancients, from Eastern Sources*, London, 1931; *An Old Moorish Lute Tutor ...*, Glasgow, 1933

Fayenz F., *I grandi del Jazz*, Milan, 1963

Fétis F. J., *Antoine Stradivari, Luthier célèbre connu sous le nom de Stradivarius*, Paris, 1856

Fissore R., *Traité de lutherie ancienne ...*, Paris, 1899

Fitzgibbon H. M., *The Story of the Flute*, London, 1914

Flade E., *Gottfried Silbermann*, Leipzig, 1953

Fleury E., *Les instruments de musique sur les monuments de Moyen-Age du Département de l'Aisne ...*, Lyons, 1882

Flood W. H. G., *The Story of the Bagpipe*, London and New York, 1911; *The Story of the Harp*, London and New York, 1905

Francoeur L. J., *Diapason général de tous les Instruments à vent*, Paris, 1792

Gábry G., *Alte Musikinstrumente*, Budapest, 1969

Gafori F., *Practica musice ...*, 1496; *Theorica musice ...* Milan, 1492; facsimile edition, Rome, 1934; *De Harmonia Instrumentorum Opus*, Milan, 1518

Galilei V., *Dialogo ... della musica antica, et della moderna*, Florence, 1602

Gallini N., *Museo civico di antichi strumenti musicali*, Milan, 1958

Galpin F. W., *The Music of the Sumerians ... the Babylonians and Assyrians*, Cambridge, 1937; *A Textbook of European Instruments*, London, 1956; *Old English Instruments of Music*, London, 1965

Ganassi S., *Opera Intitulata Fontegara*, Venice, 1535, facsimile edition, Berlin, 1959

Garnault P., *Instruments d'Amour*, Nice, 1927; *La Trompette Marine*, Nice, 1926

Gát J., *A zongora története*, Budapest, 1964

Geeringer K., *Museum Carolino Augustaeum. Sammlung alter Musikinstrumente*, Leipzig, 1932

Geist B., *Co nevíte o jazzu (The Unknown about Jazz)*, Prague, 1966

Gerbert M., *Scriptores Ecclesiastici de Musica Sacra potissimum*, St Blasien, 1784, 3 vols; facsimile edition, Milan, 1931

Gerle H., *Musica Teusch auf die Instrument ...*, Nuremberg, 1546

Gevaert F. A., *Histoire de la Musique de l'Antiquité*, Ghent, 1881; *Nouveau traité d'instrumentation*, Paris, 1885

Gilliam L. E. and Lichtenwanger W., *The Dayton C. Miller Flute Collection: A Checklist of the Instruments*, Washington, 1961

Girard A., *Histoire et richesse de la Flûte*, Paris, 1953

Glareanus H., *Dodekachordon*, Basle, 1547

Gli strumenti musicali raccolti nel Museo del R. Istituto L. Cherubini a Firenze, Florence, 1911

Goehlinger F. A., *Geschichte des Klavichords*, Basle, 1910

Goodrich W., *The Organ in France ...*, Boston, 1917

Gratia I. E., *Les instruments de musique du XXᵉ siècle*, Paris, 1931

Gressmann H., *Musik und Musikinstrumente im Alten Testament*, Giessen, 1903

Haacke W., *Orgeln in aller Welt*, Stuttgart, 1965

Hajdecki A., *Die italienische Lira da Braccio*, Mostar, 1892

Hamma F., *Meisterwerke italienischer Geigenbaukunst*, Stuttgart, n.d.

Hammerich A., *Les lurs de l'âge de bronze au Musée national de Copenhague*, Copenhagen, 1894

Harding R., *The Piano-Forte*, Cambridge, 1933

Harrison F. and Rimmer J., *European Musical Instruments*, London, 1964

Hart G., *The Violin: its Famous Makers and Imitators*, London, 1909

Haubensak Q., *Ursprung und Geschichte der Geige*, Marburg, 1930

Haweis H. R., *Old Violins*, Edinburgh, 1905

Hayes G. R., *Musical Instruments and their Music, 1500—1750. I: The Treatment of Instrumental Music*, London, 1928. *II: The Viola and other Bowed Instruments*, London, 1930

Heckel W., *Der Fagott*, Leipzig, 1931

Heinitz W., *Instrumentenkunde*, Potsdam, 1929

Helm E., *Music at the Court of Frederick The Great*, Oklahoma, 1960

Henley W., *Antonio Stradivari*, Brighton, 1961

Heron-Allen E., *Violin-making, as it was and is*, London, 1885; *De Fidiculis Bibliographia: being an Attempt towards a Bibliography of the Violin and all other Instruments played with a Bow*, London, 1890—4, 2 vols; *De Fidiculis Opuscula*, London, 1882—95, 8 vols

Herrad of Landsberg, abbot of Hohenburg, *Hortus Deliciarum*, Paris, 1879—99 and Strasbourg, 1901

Herzfeld F., *Musica Nova*, Berlin, 1954

Hickmann H., *Aegypten*, Leipzig, 1962; *45 Siècles de Musique dans l'Egypte Ancienne*, Paris, 1956

Hill W. E., *Antonio Stradivari, his Life and Work*, London, 1909; *The Violin-Makers of the Guarneri Family*, London, 1931

Hill W. E. and sons, *The Salabue Stradivari*, London, 1891

Hipkins A. J., *A Description and History of the Pianoforte and of the Older Keyboard Stringed Instruments*, London, 1896; *Musical Instruments, Historic, Rare and Unique*, Edinburgh, 1888

Hirt F. J., *Meisterwerke des Klavierbaus*, Olten, 1955

Hofmann R., *Katechismus der Musikinstrumente*, Leipzig, 1890

Huggins M. Gio, *Paolo Maggini, his Life and Work*, London, 1892

Hunt E., *The Recorder and its Music*, London, 1962
Hutter J., *Hudební nástroje (Musical Instruments)*, Prague, 1945

Idelsohn A., *Jewish Music*, New York, 1949

Jacquot A., *La Lutherie Lorraine et Française*, Paris, 1912; *La Musique instrumentale de la Renaissance*, Paris, 1955
Jahnel F., *Die Gitarre und ihr Bau*, Frankfurt, 1963
Jalovec K., *Houslaři (Violin-makers)*, Prague, 1952; *Čeští housslaři (Czech Violin-makers)*, Prague, 1959
James P., *Early Keyboard Instruments from their Beginnings to the Year 1820*, London, 1930
Jeppesen K., *Die italienische Orgelmusik am Anfang des Cinquecento*, Oslo, 1960

Kalkbrenner A., *Wilhelm Wieprecht, Direktor der sämtlichen Musikchöre des Garde-Corps, sein Leben und Werke*, Berlin, 1882
Kastner G., *Les Danses des Morts*, Paris, 1852; *La harpe d'Éole et la musique cosmique*, Paris, 1856
Katalog zu den Sammlungen des Händel-Hauses in Halle / Saale, Halle / Saale, 1966
Kinkeldey O., *Orgel und Klavier in der Musik des 16. Jahrhunderts*, Leipzig, 1910
Kinsky G., *Katalog des Musikhistorischen Museums von Wilhelm Heyer in Köln*, Cologne, 1912; *Geschichte der Musik in Bildern*, Leipzig, 1929
Kirby P. R., *The Kettle-Drums*, London, 1930
Kircher A., *Musurgia universalis*, Rome, 1650; *Phonurgia nova*, Campinae, 1673; *Neue Hall- und Ton-Kunst*, Nördlingen, 1684
Körte O., *Laute und Lautenmusik bis zur Mitte des 16. Jahrhunderts*, Leipzig, 1901
Kool J., *Das Saxophon*, Leipzig, 1931
Kuna M. and Pleva L., *Foukací harmonika (Mouth Organ)*, Prague, 1960
Kunsthistorisches Museum, Wien. Katalog der Sammlung alter Musikinstrumente. I: Saitenklaviere, Vienna, 1966
Kunze S., *Die Instrumentalmusik Giovanni Gabrielis*, Tutzing, 1963

Lanfranco G. M., *Scintille di musica*, Brescia, 1533
Langwill L. G., *An Index of Musical Wind-Instrument Makers*, Edinburgh, 1962; *The Bassoon and Contrabassoon*, London, 1965
Layer A., *Matthias Klotz von Mittenwald*, Feldafing/Obb, 1959
Leblanc H., *Verteidigung der Viola da Gamba gegen die Angriffe der Violine und die Anmassung des Violoncellos*, Kassel, 1951
Leonhardt K., *Geigenbau und Klangfrage*, Frankfurt, 1963
Levy J., *Die Signalinstrumente in den altfranzösischen Texten*, Halle, 1910
Lütgendorff W., *Die Geigen-und Lautenmacher vom Mittelalter bis zur Gegenwart*, Frankfurt, 1922, 2 vols
Luscinius O., *Musurgia seu Praxis Musicae*, Strasbourg, 1536

Mace T., *Musick's Monument*, London, 1676; facsimile edition, Paris, 1958
Mahillon V. C., *Catalogue descriptif et analytique du Musée instrumental du Conservatoire royal de Musique*, 5 vols, Ghent, 1893—1922; *Instruments à vent. I: Le Trombone, son histoire, sa théorie, sa construction. II: Le Cor. III: La Trompette*, Brussels, 1906—7
Mahrenholz C., *Die Berechnung der Orgelpfeifenmensuren vom Mittelalter bis zur Mitte des 19. Jahrhunderts*, Kassel, 1938
Majer J. F. B. K., *Museum musicum*, Nuremberg, 1741; facsimile edition, Kassel, 1954
Malson L., *Histoire du jazz moderne*, Paris, 1961
Manessesche Liederhandschrift, facsimile edition, Leipzig, 1924-7
Manson W. L., *The Highland Bagpipe*, Paisley and London, 1901
Mařák J. and Nopp V., *Housle (Violin)*, Prague, 1941
Marcuse S., *Musical Instruments at Yale*, Yale, 1960: *Musical Instruments: A Comprehensive Dictionary*, New York, 1964
Martin C., *La Musique électronique*, Paris, 1950
Mason D. G., *The Orchestral Instruments and what they do*, New York, 1909
Mattheson J., *Das neu-eröffnete Orchester*, Hamburg, 1713
Menke W., *History of the Trumpet of Bach and Handel*, London, 1934
Méreaux A., *Les clavecinistes de 1637 à 1790. Histoire du clavecin*, Paris, n. d.
Mersenne M., *Harmonie universelle*, Paris, 1636
Mertens C., *Concrete en Electronische Muziek*, Brussels, 1957

Metropolitan Museum of Art. Catalogue of the Crosby Brown Collection of Musical Instruments of All Nations, New York, 1904
Meyer — Eppler W., *Elektrische Klangerzeugung*, Bonn, 1949
Miller D. C., *The Flute and Flute-Playing . . .*, Cleveland, 1908
Mikšovský J., *Václav František Červený*, Český Brod, 1896
Modr A., *Hudební nástroje (Musical Instruments)*, Prague, 1954
Moles A., *Les Musiques expérimentales*, Paris, 1960
Möller M., *The Violin-Makers of the Low Countries*, Amsterdam, 1955
Morley-Pegge R., *The French Horn*, London, 1960
Mustel A., *L'orgue expressif*, Paris, 1903

Nagy L., *Az aquincumi orgona*, Budapest, 1934
Nef K., *Historisches Museum Basel. Katalog IV: Musikinstrumente*, Basle, 1906; *Geschichte unserer Musikinstrumente*, Leipzig, 1926
Němec V., *Pražské varhany (Prague Organs)*, Prague, 1944
Neupert H., *Das Cembalo*, Kassel, 1956; *Vom Musikstab zum modernen Klavier*, Kassel, 1960
Niederheitmann F., *Cremona*, Leipzig, 1928
Nordlind T., *Systematik der Saiteninstrumente. I: Geschichte der Zither*, Stockholm, 1936; *II: Geschichte des Klaviers*, Hanover, 1939
Novák P., *Bici nástroje v teorii a praxi (Percussion Instruments in Theory and Practice)*, Ostrava, 1956

Œuvre collective, *Das Akkordeon*, Leipzig, 1964
Ott A., *Ausstellung 'Alte Musik'*, Munich, 1951
Otto I., *Das Musikinstrumenten-Museum Berlin*, Berlin, 1968

Panum H., *The Stringed Instruments of the Middle Ages*, London, 1940
Parent M., *Les instruments de Musique au XIVᵉ siècle*, Paris, 1925
Pedrell F., *Emporio cientifico é histórico de organografía musical antigua española*, Barcelona, 1901
Pierre C., *La facture instrumentale à l'Exposition universelle de 1889*, Paris, 1890; *Les Facteurs d'Instruments de Musique*, Paris, 1893
Piersig F., *Die Einführung des Hornes in die Kunstmusik . . .*, Halle, 1927
Pincherle M., *Feuillets d'histoire du violon*, Paris, 1927
Pirro A., *Les Clavecinistes*, Paris, n. d.
Pougin A., *Le violon, les violonistes et la musique du XVIᵉ au XVIIIᵉ siècle*, Paris, 1924
Praetorius M., *Syntagma Musicum. II: De Organographia*, Wolfenbüttel, 1619; facsimile edition, Kassel, 1958
Pulver J., *A Dictionary of Old English Music and Musical Instruments*, London, 1923

Quantz J. J., *Versuch einer Anweisung die Flöte traversiere zu spielen*, Berlin, 1752
Quoika R., *Die altösterreichische Orgel*, Kassel, 1941

Racek J., *Hudební nástroje v dějinném vývoji lidské společnosti (Musical Instruments in the Historical Evolution of Human Society)*, Brno, 1953
Ramos de Pareja B., *De Musica Tractatus, sive Musica Practica . . .*, Bononiae, 1482
Reese C., *Music in the Middle Ages*, New York, 1940; *Music in the Renaissance*, New York, 1954
Rendall F., *The Clarinet*, London, 1957
Rensch R., *The Harp*, New York, 1950
Richardson E. G., *The Acoustics of Orchestral Instruments and of the Organ*, London, 1929
Riehm W., *Das Harmonium, sein Bau und seine Behandlung*, Berlin, 1897
Riemann H., *Katechismus der Musikinstrumente*, Leipzig, 1888
Ritchie H., *The Dulcimer Book*, New York, 1963
Ritter H., *Die Geschichte der Viola Alta*, Leipzig, 1877
Rockstro R. S., *A Treatise on the Construction, the History and the Practice of the Flute . . .*, London, 1928
Rödig J., *Geigenbau in neuer Zeit*, Frankfurt, 1966
Rousseau J., *Traité de la viole*, Paris, 1687; facsimile edition, Amsterdam, 1965
Roussel A. and König A., *Grundlagen der Geige und des Geigenbaues*, Frankfurt, 1965
Rubardt P., *Führer durch das Musikinstrumenten-Museum*, Leipzig, 1955

271

Rühlmann J., *Die Geschichte der Bogeninstrumente. Text und Atlas*, Brunswick, 1882
Rupp E., *Die Entwicklungsgeschichte der Orgelbaukunst*, Einsiedeln, 1929
Rushworth-Dreaper, *Collection of Antique Musical Instruments and Historical Manuscripts*, Liverpool, 1932
Rusell R., *The Harpsichord and Clavichord*, London, 1959; *Victoria and Albert Museum. Catalogue of Musical Instruments. I:Keyboard Instruments*, London, 1968
Ruth-Sommer H., *Alte Musikinstrumente*, Berlin, 1920
Rychlík J., *Žešťové nástroje bez strojiva (Brass Instruments without Mechanisms)*, Prague, 1960; *Pověry a problémy jazzu (Superstitions and Problems of Jazz)*, Prague, 1959

Sachs C., *Reallexikon der Musikinstrumente . . .*, Berlin, 1913; *Sammlung alter Musikinstrumente bei der staatlichen Hochschule für Musik zu Berlin*, Berlin, 1922; *Die Musikinstrumente*, Břeclav, 1923; *Das Klavier*, Berlin, 1923; *Geist und Werden der Musikinstrumente*, Berlin, 1929; *Handbuch der Musikinstrumentenkunde*, Leipzig, 1930; *The History of Musical Instruments*, London, 1942
Salinas F., *De Musica Libri Septem . . .*, Samananca, 1577
Sandys W. and Forster A. A., *The History of the Violin and other Instruments Played with the Bow . . .*, London, 1864
Seewald O., *Beiträge zur Kenntnis der steinzeitlichen Musikinstrumente Europas*, Vienna, 1934
Seifers H., *Systematik der Blasinstrumente*, Frankfurt, 1967
Senn W., *Jakob Stainer, der Geigenmacher zu Absam*, Innsbruck, 1951
Sharpe A. P., *The Story of the Spanish Guitar*, London, 1954
Schaeffner A., *Les Origines des Instruments de Musique*, Paris, 1936
Schafhäutl K. E., *Die Musikinstrumente. Bericht der Beurteilungscomission bei der allgemeinen deutschen Industrie-Ausstellung in München, 1854*, Munich, 1855
Schlesinger K., *The Instruments of the Modern Orchestra and Early Records of the Precursors of the Violin Family*, London, 1910; *The Greek Aulos*, London, 1939
Schlick A., *Spiegel der Orgelmacher und Organisten*, Heidelberg, 1511; new edition, Kassel, 1951
Schlosser J., *Die Sammlung alter Musikinstrumente*, Vienna, 1920; *Unsere Musikinstrumente: Eine Einführung in ihre Geschichte*, Vienna, 1922
Schmitz H., *Querflöte und Querflötenspiel*, Kassel, 1952
Schneider W., *Historisch-technische Beschreibung der musikalischen Instrumente . . .*, Leipzig, 1834
Schubert F. L., *Alle gebräuchlichen Musikinstrumente, in alphabetischer Ordnung*, Leipzig, n. d.; *Katechismus der Musikinstrumente*, Leipzig, 1862; *Die Blechinstrumente der Musik*, Leipzig, 1866
Schultz H., *Instrumentenkunde*, Leipzig, 1931
Skinner W., *The Belle Skinner Collection of Old Musical Instruments, Holyoke, Massachusetts*, Massachusetts, 1933
Sommer H., *Die Laute in ihrer musikgeschichtlichen kultur- und kunsthistorischen Bedeutung*, Berlin, 1920
Speer D., *Grund-richtiger, kurz, leicht und nöthiger Unterricht der musicalischen Kunst*, Ulm, 1687
Spillane D., *The Piano*, New York, 1907
Stainer C. A., *A Dictionary of Violin Makers*, London, 1896
Stanley A. A., *Catalogue of the Stearns Collection of Musical Instruments*, Michigan, 1918
Stearns M. W., *The Story of Jazz*, New York, 1958
Stockhausen K., *Texte zur elektronischen und instrumentalen Musik*, Cologne, 1959
Straeten W. van der, *The History of the Violoncello, the Viol da Gamba, their Precursors*, London, 1915; *The History of the Violin*, London, 1933; *The Romance of the Fiddle . . .*, London, 1911
Stüwen W., *Orgel und Orgelbauer im halleschen Land vor 1800*, Wiesbaden, 1964
Sumuer W. K., *The Pianoforte*, London, 1966

Terry C. S., *Bach's Orchestra*, London, 1932
Teuchert E. and Haupt E. W., *Musik-Instrumentenkunde*, Leipzig, 1910
The Ridley Collection of Musical Wind Instruments, Luton, 1957
Tinctoris, *De Inventione et Usu Musicae*, Naples, 1487
Trautwein F., *Elektrische Musik*, Berlin, 1930
Travers E., *Les instruments de musique au XIVe siècle d'après Guillaume de Machault*, Paris, 1882
Treder D., *Die Musikinstrumente in den höfischen Epen der Blütezeit*, Greifswald, 1933
Trichet P. and Lesure F., *Traité des Instruments de musique*, 1640; new edition, Neuilly-sur-Seine, 1957

Utrecht Psalter, facsimile edition, London, 1875

Vadding M. and Merseburger M., *Das Violoncello und seine Literatur*, Leipzig, 1920
Valdrighi L. F., *Nomocheliurgographia antica e moderna . . .*, Modena, 1881
Vannes R., *Dictionnaire Universel des Luthiers*, Brussels, 1951
Velebný K., *Jazzová praktika (Jazz Practice)*, Prague, 1967
Vërtkov K. A., *Russkaja rogovaja muzika*, Moscow, 1948
Vidal F., *Lou Tambourin*, Aix, 1864
Vidal L. A., *Les Instruments à archet . . .*, Paris, 1876, 3 vols
Virdung S., *Musica getutscht . . .*, Basle, 1511; facsimile edition, Kassel, 1931

Wantzloeben S., *Das Monochord als Instrument und als System*, Halle, 1911
Wasielewski W. J., *Die Violine im XVII. Jahrhundert und die Instrumentalcomposition*, Bonn, 1874; *Geschichte der Instrumentalmusik im XVI. Jahrhundert*, Berlin, 1878; *The Violoncello and its History*, London, 1894; *Die Violine und ihre Meister*, Leipzig, 1910
Wasserbauer I. et al., *Jazzový slovník (Jazz Dictionary)*, Bratislava, 1966
Weigel J. C., *Musicalisches Theatrum*, 1720; facsimile edition, Kassel, 1964
Weiss J., *Die musikalischen Instrumente des Alten Testaments*, Prague, 1895
Welch C., *History of the Boehm Flute*, London 1896; new edition, New York, 1961; *Six Lectures on the Recorder*, London, 1911
Welcker H., *Neu eröffnetes Magazin musikalischer Tonwerkzeuge*, Frankfurt, 1855
Wessely O., *Die Musikinstrumenten-Sammlung*, Linz, 1952
Wetzger P., *Die Flöte*, Heilbronn, n. d.
Willemin N. X., *Choix de . . . instruments de musique*, Paris, 1839, 2 vols
Winternitz E. and Stunzi L., *Die schönsten Musikinstrumente des Abendlandes*, Munich, 1966
de Wit P., *Die Perlen aus der Instrumenten-Sammlung von Paul de Wit in Leipzig*, Leipzig, 1892; *Katalog des Musikhistorischen Museums von Paul de Wit*, Leipzig, 1903
Wörthmüller W., *Die Nürnberger Trompeten- und Posaunenmacher des 17. und 18. Jahrhunderts*, Nuremberg, 1955
Wood G. B., *Musical Instruments in York Castle Museum*, York, n. d.

Yorke-Long A., *Music at Court*, London, 1954
Young T. C., *The Making of Musical Instruments*, London, 1939
Youssoupov N. B., *Luthomonographie historique et raisonnée. Essai sur l'histoire du violon et sur les ouvrages des anciens luthiers célèbres . . .*, Munich 1856

Zacconi L., *Prattica di musica . . . divisa in quattro libri*, Venice, 1596
Zamminger F., *Die Musik und musikalischen Instrumente in ihrer Beziehung zu Gesetzen der Akustik*, Giessen, 1855
Zarlino G., *Di tutte l'opere del R. M. Gioseffo Zarlino . . .*, Venice 1588—9, 4 vols

INDEX OF MUSICAL INSTRUMENTS

Page numbers in roman refer to the text
Numbers in italics refer to illustrations

This book is a completely new edition of a work first published in 1956 by the eminent musicologist Dr. Alexander Buchner, who has revised and re-illustrated the entire content throughout, and also now includes jazz and electric musical instruments.

As Dr. Buchner remarks in his Introduction, nothing evokes the sound of an instrument as vividly as the shape and design of the instrument itself. Musical instruments just ask to be pictured and the sight of them immediately calls to mind a certain sound. Yet no other branch of musical knowledge has been so neglected as the history of musical instruments, and too few of the small number of works available on this subject contain sufficiently detailed illustrations.

This present book, on the other hand, describes the development of musical instruments in pictures without lengthy text. The illustrations – 300 in black and white, 31 in color and 21 line drawings – will speak for themselves to those who love the art of musical sound and the musical instruments that transform such sound into audible reality.